THEY CALL ME THE BACON PRIEST

Werenfried van Straaten

They Call Me
the
Bacon Priest

IGNATIUS PRESS   SAN FRANCISCO

Title of the German original:
Sie nemen mich Speckpater
© 1961, 1989 Georg Bitter Verlag KG
Original English editions:
N.V. Drukkerig de Spaarnestad, Haarlem, 1961 (first edition)
New City Press, 1965 (second edition)
Augustine Publishing Company, 1981 (third edition)

Cover by Riz Boncan Marsella

With ecclesiastical approval
Revised American edition
© 1991 Aid to the Church in Need
All rights reserved
ISBN 0-89870-276-3
Library of Congress catalogue number 89-81006
Printed in the United States of America

CONTENTS

FOREWORD

Standing at the doors of St. Peter's as we bishops streamed out from the Vatican Council was this white-robed Canon. He wasn't visibly holding up the basilica. He was holding up the charity of Christ, which presses on the whole Church (2 Cor 5:14).

A blessing on those burly shoulders!

I heard that the physical strain on him has recently taken its toll. So the burden of the world's distress can shatter even giants. This giant, because of his age and medical condition, depends more than ever on his bene-factors, whom he urges to even greater efforts.

Do help him to keep up the relentless pressure of the charity of Christ! This book would well serve its purpose if it wins prayers for his health and alms for the Church in Need.

✠ Thomas Holland
Bishop of Salford
28 March 1980

FOREWORD TO THE 1961 EDITION

You have to like him, this headstrong Fleming, this herald of uncompromising Christian neighbourly love, this valiant conqueror of national antipathies, Fr. Werenfried van Straaten.

It must have been towards the end of the 1940s when I met him for the first time in Königstein, Germany. Straight-away he told me about his experience in Vinkt, and I was captivated both by what he said and by his way of recounting it. This was an incorrigible optimist speaking, convinced that men were better than they were made out to be; all one had to do was to find the right word to inspire them and they would be ready to make any sacrifice. This was a man with a heart of gold, humourous and sensitive, a modest and profoundly pious priest and monk. Once I called him a modern Genghis-Khan, because wherever he had been there was nothing left; and he did not take it amiss.

May God preserve his heart of gold and let him continue working for the good of the thousands who suffer in body and in soul.

> Cologne, Feast of St. Francis of Assisi 1961
> ✠ Joseph Cardinal Frings
> Archbishop of Cologne

HOW IT ALL BEGAN

It was December 1947, and the clock struck three in the morning as I finished my article in time for the Christmas number of the abbey magazine. That article was to decide my future.

I was thirty-four years old. Until then I had been an unknown Norbertine, with a weak constitution, who sang a little too loudly and slightly out of tune in choir. I conducted retreats in convents and boarding schools, but my main job was as secretary to our abbot, the unforgettable Emilius Stalmans. Every month I wrote an article for the abbey magazine: in those turbulent years after the Second World War, these articles occasionally got me into trouble with the ecclesiastical censor, a kindly old Canon in Malines (since gone to his rest). He did his best to smooth down my inopportune scribblings and was always a little sad when he was obliged to strike out one of my fine-sounding phrases. In his heart of hearts he agreed with me, but the burden of his years had made him wiser and more circumspect. From him I learned a little diplomacy and a great deal of submission to ecclesiastical authority: both qualities were later to be of great value to me.

The essay I wrote that night was called "No Room at the Inn". It was, I thought, a good article, perhaps because I had borrowed a few thoughts and expressions from the well-known Dutch radio preacher Henri de Greeve—a courageous man, with eyes and heart open to all the distress that came his way. I had a great affection for him, as I did for Carl Sonnenschein and Father van Sante . . . and good Father van Clé, who, after my stormy student days, had piloted me into the safe harbour of Tongerlo. To these zealous men I owed a great deal, and I thought it no sin to make their words my own.

My first impressions of post-war Germany had been gained from a lecture by Henri de Greeve, which moved me so deeply that I was inspired to write in my Christmas article:

> Eighty miles to the east lies a town in ruins. Almost the only thing still standing is a gigantic air-raid shelter, a bunker, like those the Germans built everywhere to protect the population from the bombings. All the poor people of the town who still remain alive dwell in this one bunker. Thousands are crowded together in pestilential stench. Each family, insofar as they can still be called families, lies huddled together on a few square yards of concrete. Here there is neither fire nor warmth, other than the warmth of bodies crowded together. Among these people, too, Christ seeks to dwell in His purity, His love and goodness. The shepherds worshipped Christ in a stable, but these people do not even have a stable. By human standards Christ cannot live there. There is no room for Him.

This was how we began our appeal to the readers of the abbey magazine for help for the defeated Germans. The results exceeded all expectations: "Aid to Eastern Priests" (as Aid to the Church in Need was known at first) was born overnight, as convoys of charity from Flanders began their trek to the East.

PLATE 1. Father Werenfried walks through the gateway of Tongerlo Abbey and out into the big, wide world. In 1947 the Abbot General of the Premonstratensian Order, Msgr. Hubertus Noots, had asked Abbot Emilius Stalmans to entrust his young confrere Werenfried with a special relief campaign for the exiled priests and Catholics in Germany.

Abbot Noots, who was then the Norbertine Abbot General, read of my appeal in Rome and sent a contribution. Then, when the refugee Bishop Kindermann came knocking on his door for help a few months later, the old Abbot General remembered his young fellow-Norbertine in Tongerlo. He contacted Abbot Stalmans, asking him to give me permission to organise a special relief project in support of the three thousand German priests and their six million faithful, who would otherwise die utterly isolated, rootless in a foreign land.

There were enormous difficulties to be overcome. Aid to Eastern Priests was accused of acting for political motives. A Brussels priest who had become unbalanced from years in a concentration camp vilified me in public; victims of the German terror protested that I was carrying charity beyond the bounds of reason.

By February 1948, I was compelled to take up my pen and defend myself:

> Charity does not mean fine-sounding phrases: it means deeds and sacrifices. It claims a part of ourselves. It requires of us a personal attitude toward the starving, the naked, the sick and those in prison, and all others in whom Christ is hidden and of whom He spoke when describing the Day of Judgment. Charity also demands that we acknowledge and assist Christ even in those who, through the fault of warmongers, wear the uniform of the enemy. These are still our brethren, for Christ has called them, too, to be children of the same heavenly Father. Now these, the poorest of our brethren, are in the deepest distress, and we cannot, with impunity, close our eyes to this fact. Those who can turn their heads away from so much suffering are not worthy of

the name Christian. We know that these lines may be falsely interpreted, but it will not stop us from saying this much: in spite of the fact that so many wives and mothers among us are still sorrowing for their dear ones who fell in the German outrage, yet we dare to pray to God that He may grant them heroic strength, super-human fortitude, in order to forget their agony and to turn their tear-stained eyes with motherly love to the suffering Germans and to understand, as only mothers can understand, and to forgive, as only a woman can forgive . . .

God heard this prayer, and through His grace many thousands found the strength to forgive. There were women who gave away the clothes their husbands had worn before the Germans had taken them away to be shot. Other people who had lost health, happiness and children under the German reign of terror volunteered to become my assistants. In Vinkt, Belgium, where in 1940 eighty-five men and boys were massacred by the invading Germans, the people now *retaliated* with gifts of loving kindness. Waves of mercy and love swept through Flanders and soon flooded the Netherlands as well.

ENCOUNTER WITH DISTRESS

I received valuable support from an elderly Capuchin, Father Valerius Claes, who fought with indomitable spirit under the banners of his "Catholic Unity" for solidarity with German Catholics. With his aid I was soon able to make my first journey to Germany, thus obtaining the material for the sermons and lectures that I gave continuously in my attempt to arouse hearts and consciences in Flanders.

This was not difficult, for, by God's will, I was brutally confronted during my first travels in Germany with such distress that for years I was unable to speak of it without the deepest emotion. My personal experiences in the rubble of Cologne and the bunkers of Frankfurt, which I related a thousand times to horrified audiences, helped me greatly to open eyes, hearts and purses in aid of brothers in need.

Never shall I forget the impression made on me by the visit to a *Hochbunker*. Black and square rose the monstrous building against the bright summer sky. A dark block of concrete, as large as a factory, with two gaping mouths, like the god of destruction reigning over all the ruins of Germany, it was the modern Moloch to which the helpless children of our times were sacrificed, the new Beast threatening Christianity. In the places where the churches had been swept away by war, these monsters had remained standing. Black as the night, they devoured by the hundreds of thousands those who, by the terms of the Potsdam Agreement, were doomed to exile.

After my visit to this bunker, I wrote, horrified:

Listen to the despairing sighs of the exiles, thrown like devils' fodder into the mouths of the shelters. They dwell so far behind the three-foot-thick concrete walls that their presence is hardly noticed. But they have been billeted on the devil.

Enter this den of iniquity, pass into this black Beast with white entrails, penetrate into its deepest belly, full of drab human fragments. It is a beast of prey. From hall to hall, from floor to floor, upstairs and downstairs, the poisonous glands of the monster are everywhere at work. The digestive system can be seen everywhere, in the smell of decay and the despair of those who are helplessly devoured alive, sucked dry, crushed to pieces until they dissolve into a bestial, unspeakable human pulp.

What a black page in the history of the Church! Here outcast Christians are huddled together in nakedness and squalour. Four families, chosen at random, are cast into each concrete cave. Sixteen beds or more fill the available space. There is no room for tables and chairs. Nowhere any feeling of home or family life. No privacy. Everywhere lustful eyes, lewd gestures, indecent talk, wanton laughter. There is nothing you can do about it. Living in herds destroys all sense of decency.

Here families with four, five or six children gradually waste away, sallow, shrivelled babies alongside grandmothers of eighty, in an oppressive stench of sweat and fetid air. There are no windows. For years there has been nothing but the sooty light of candles and torches. There are no lamps, and those who live here develop

PLATE 2. A high-rise bunker in post-war Germany. Grey and feature-less, this monstrosity in Frankfurt-Höchst rises up against the gentle summer breeze. Originally built as air-raid shelters, these concrete blocks were used as emergency billets for refugees and those who had lost their homes in the bombings.

weak eyes and can no longer bear the sunlight. Consumptives spit into a basin. Old people in their dotage wallow in their own filth. Children crawl under the beds, in the narrow passages and up and down the concrete staircases. These anemic children are dreadful to see—pale and transparent, with precocious eyes and a piteous smile on their aged faces.

Once every twelve hours, ventilators suck fresh air into the bunker for fifteen minutes. But the monster's breathing is hardly noticeable. Parched throats gasp in vain for air for their lungs, and the wretches who stumble and fall seven times a day hope in vain for purity for their souls.

How hopeless is the fight against unchecked sin, here where there are no walls to preserve chastity. How can virtue take root where twenty, forty, seventy men and girls, women and boys, children and old people live together, sleep together, sweat, dress and undress and follow the call of nature for months and years on end in these hot concrete caverns? This is hell for body and soul. It is the realm of confusion, egoism and the brutal law of the jungle. Every foot of concrete is wrestled for as women elbow each other away from the cooking stoves. Here life is thwarted of all it can lawfully lay claim to, and, in revenge, it bursts all bonds, gorges itself on sin and grasps with greedy talons all the passion and false joy that enter the concrete shelter from the roaring city.

It is a long journey through these God-forsaken bowels, this endless maze of passages and stairways. The whitewashed concrete is oppressive. It is difficult to breathe, and the hot air weighs on the chest like lead. Sweat pours down as we stumble on. One would like to curse and run away from this misery. The mind revolts at all it sees and hears, finding no answers to it all. Everywhere the same tragic story, with countless variations of sorrow and humiliation, and, like a refrain, always the same painful question: "When are we going back home?"

Home is the only thing these outcasts have left to cling to. Do we dare deprive them of this hope? Yet it is just an illusion, for East Prussia, so they say, is now peopled with Tartars and Khirgiz; in Silesia the fields are reverting to steppes, while in Sudetenland bulldozers are rumbling over two hundred and twenty-five villages and razing them to the ground, as there are no Czechs to dwell in them.

Dear God, You Who made the sun and the wide spaces and the winds and the soft rains to freshen the air, is there not room for all? Why must these outcast millions, these pariahs, be without Your light and Your fresh air? Why have they been deprived of a human existence? Why should not the policy of the victorious Powers be favourable to these afflicted people, to women and children who have done nothing to deserve such a fate? Why must the people expiate the crimes committed by the state? It is the state and not the people that unchains war—a wild beast of prey that devours its own people as well as those of other states. This atrocity, this destruction, was not necessary. It was a crime, and madness, to hunt sixteen million people to death or sell them into slavery, to chase them into ruins and concrete bunkers and then burn or destroy their houses; crime and madness to plant forests on arable land, to condemn the millions who reclaimed these fertile fields from the wilderness to starve among the ruins of bombed cities. O God, You Who once looked down upon the misery of Job and saved Jonah from the belly of the whale, look

PLATE 3. A widow in a Frankfurt bunker. Six years behind metre-thick concrete in a fetid room with no windows or ventilation. Her husband died here.

down now upon the affliction of Your people and deliver them from the belly of the Beast. . . .

But the Lord will not work through miracles. Though He remains merciful in all eternity, He has allotted the works of His mercy to us who are His children. Whether the name of the Lord is blessed or cursed in these abodes depends on us.

How niggardly we have been with our charity. If Christians had but a faint idea of Christ's Mystical Body—if we had felt even the slightest bit of solidarity with our brothers delivered into the hands of the Beast—storms of protest would have cried to heaven long ago and caravans of relief would have crossed the world. But Divine Love has become a stranger on earth!

Turn within yourself and look God in the eyes. Would you dare to look your own father in the face if you had allowed your brothers and sisters to perish without raising a hand to help them? Think, then, of God's wrath if you have not done everything you can to alleviate the suffering of His children.

Listen. If there is any Christianity left in the West, the day must come when we can set out for the East, flying the standard of consolation and love. But meanwhile, in Germany, the Good Shepherds and the Good Samaritans and the gentle angels of love who follow their lost sheep deep into the belly of the Beast, weeping bitter tears, are dying by the score. They visit their flocks, they bless and console them, but their hands are empty.

The least we can do is to keep these Samaritans alive and give them something that will relieve the worst distress. So for the love of Christ give of your plenty or of your poverty to help those priests from behind the Iron Curtain.

This is how I wrote and spoke during those first months and years of ACN, even to the tiniest villages of Flanders. At first I had to go and find my audience: I went to meet them during the lunch break at the factory gate. I spoke at meetings or tea parties of country guilds and women's institutes. I stood by the roadside in my white habit until a factory owner would give me a lift in his Cadillac, so that I could rouse him with my shocking news. I went from school to school to ask for the children's prayers, a piece of chocolate and the contents of their money-boxes for the Church in distress.

The campaign grew like lightning. Monsignor Cruysberghs, chairman of the Farmers' Union, helped me by word and deed (and especially with the authority of his purple) to collect bacon and grain from farmers' wives. Canon Dubois placed first of all the Catholic Students' Action, and then himself, at the disposal of the project to obtain a "vehicle for God". We raised pigs in Flanders and lambs in the Netherlands for the displaced Germans. We mobilised Flemish schoolchildren to adopt three thousand itinerant priests: three thousand schools and school years each had their own priest for whom they prayed and sacrificed their pocket money and to whom, for years, they offered the heart-warming consolation of their simple letters.

Through the adoption of these priests, who received a monthly parcel of provisions and a letter from their little benefactors that was promptly answered, ACN became a popular institution. Through this personal correspondence not only the school children but also their fathers and mothers, uncles and aunts became involved in the problems with which our work was faced. Fifteen tons of food a month were sent in ten-pound parcels to German Iron Curtain priests during the first couple of years. This helped them to stay alive and enabled them to back up their difficult apostolate among the despairing exiles with gifts—showing love with deeds.

A NEW NAME

It will never be forgotten that the real origin of ACN lay in the hearts of the Flemish peasants. It was they who furnished the initial capital of this enterprise when they unhesitatingly took part in the great Battle of the Bacon of 1948.

After my first encounter with the distress of defeated Germany, I returned to the abbey deeply shocked. On my arrival I found that a retreat for priests was being held. I was invited to give a talk, and I spoke for an hour and a half on the subject that filled my mind and heart. At the end I went round with my hat and took my first collection for my co-workers. This hat was later to become famous for the millions it collected. Some of the priests present asked me to come and preach on the subject in their parishes. One of these invitations included a tea party at the local Women's Institute. This pious society was celebrating its golden jubilee, and, besides cakes and tarts and thick ham-and-cheese sandwiches, the farmers' wives felt the need of an official speaker. I was invited to enlighten the well-to-do agri-cultural circles on the subject of the bitter distress suf-fered in Germany.

I must have spoken well that afternoon. One hundred and fifty well-nourished country women forgot the fragrant coffee urns and the piles of tasty food and shed tears of pity for the hard fate of their sorely afflicted former enemies. When I ended my barrage on their tender country hearts, there was dead silence. Even the priest could not utter a word for the tears rolling down his cheeks. As nobody spoke, I rose once more and declared encouragingly that the time had now come for the collection. Parish priest and farmers' wives unanimously nodded their agreement, but then a better idea suddenly struck me. I proposed that each of those present should take a not-too-small piece of bacon out of the chimney and deliver it to the presbytery some time in the next few days. At the end of the week I would come with the car to collect it. Everyone consented, and the Battle of the Bacon had begun. In this first parish I collected more than a ton of bacon. The first parish priest told the story to others, and soon not a week passed without my speaking two or three times at the tea parties of country guilds.

Monsignor Cruysberghs came to listen to my narrative and suggested that we extend the venture throughout the whole of Flanders. He introduced me at the regional meetings of the district heads, and supported my appeal with the whole weight of his authority and his eloquence.

Thus began my tours through the villages and hamlets of Flanders. I took Mr. Vercammen, a good friend of the abbey, zig-zagging across the map with me. Evening after evening we returned home with eight or ten hundredweight of salted bacon and a hatful of money, until at last the poor old Peugeot was sagging through its springs. Truckloads of bacon came from Flanders and Limburg and were unloaded before the astonished eyes of abbey visitors to be handed over to Brother Porter. A cold storage room was found beside the kitchen, and the bacon was piled into it until it reached the ceiling. Armed with carving knives, the novices of Tongerlo struggled through a mountain of bacon every week. They cut it down to size, wrapped it in grease-proof paper and then packed it into boxes and cases and sent it to Germany via the Catholic organisation *Caritas*. This was the beginning of the great Battle of the Bacon, to which hundreds of Iron Curtain priests and thousands of children owed their good health and perhaps their lives.

To the great indignation of my mother and to the horror of many good souls brought up to respect the priesthood, this action procured me a new name. At a mass meeting in Turnhout a farmer's wife of enormous proportions called me, for the first time, the "bacon priest". A Catholic weekly printed this name in capitals over an interview, and suddenly everyone knew about ACN.

I must admit that this name was of great help to me among the butchers and drovers with whom I maintained the most friendly relations during the first years of ACN—for the calorie problems of the German refugees were, of course, not solved by a single collection of bacon. Besides, a bacon campaign could be held only in winter, as the bacon would go bad in the summer during the weeks of transport. So a new campaign was decided upon: every Flemish farmer received a letter requesting him to fatten a pig and reserve part of it for ACN. Each reserved pig was branded in a special way and raised to the dignity of "church pig". When the moment for slaughtering it arrived, the officials at the slaughterhouse registered the number of the "church pig" and automatically booked the value of its belly and sides to the bank account we had running for this purpose with the Farmers' Union. We received, therefore, not bacon but large sums of money, with which we afterwards bought hundreds of tons of bacon when it was cheap. This was put in cold storage at Ostend.

Then I opened negotiations with the fellows of the meat and cattle trade at the Antwerp slaughterhouse. They taught me to drink a little—and also how to use a few swear words effectively. Here I managed to buy large quantities of frozen horse-meat from Argentina for practically nothing. I discovered a meat canner willing to turn this mass of meat and fat into Dutch pork sausage with a fat content of fifty-two percent. Then I discovered someone else who was willing to supply us with tin, free of charge. In this way we could provide Iron Curtain priests and refugee camps with hundreds of thousands of tins of canned meat, winter and summer.

It is not surprising that during those years I found myself obliged to become thoroughly acquainted with all details of pig breeding. This brought me into continual contact with Brother Dominic, the experienced farmer who ruled the abbey farm with a firm hand. In the course of long conversations in cowshed and pigsty, he patiently trained me in the branch of science that my new name had forced me to acquire. Only in this way could I negotiate as an equal with the men of the slaughterhouses and the canning factories, who are impressed more by expert knowledge than by piety.

During one of these discussions with Brother Dominic, a Dutch journalist rang the bell at the abbey gate

PLATE 4. Refugee children in a transit camp.

and asked for me. I was told afterwards that the dialogue ran as follows:

"I would like to speak to the bacon priest."

"You'll find him in the pigsty."

"But I don't know what he looks like."

"He'll be wearing a biretta."

Since those days, ACN has carried on numerous activities in other fields, acquiring for me other names and other titles. But I have always preferred the name "bacon priest" because it reminds me of the unsophisticated country women who were my first allies and to whom I feel myself bound in bacon and gratitude.

THE HOUSE OF EXILE

In November 1948, when ACN was almost a year old, I paid my first visit to Königstein, the place which was to play such an important part in the development of our work. Its peaceful valley was an oasis in the German desert. After the miserable journey through rubble and ruins, we found the sun shining once more on meadows. The path of destruction, it is true, led still further through cities and villages, but behind the undulating hilltops of the Taunus reigned the peace of paradise. The war had spared this valley; and the bright patchwork of green and brown fields lay on the slopes as tidily as ever, and the shaggy fleece of the pine woods still hung motionless on the brow of the hills.

Through Nassau, about fifteen miles north of Frankfurt, runs the ancient *limes*, the frontier wall of the Roman Empire. Centuries have passed since the ground rumbled under the feet of the cohorts, and since that time much has happened. The fortress became a romantic ruin, and as the last of the legions vanished, the valley was filled with a heavenly peace. Even the boldest plans can come to fruition in a climate of silence, and so Königstein, in the early post-war years, became once more a border stronghold and the launching point for an attack on the realms of darkness. It was more than a coincidence, surely, that the seminary for displaced Germans was set up in an old barracks; more than a coincidence that most of the seminarians I found there in 1948 were still dressed in worn-out uniforms. At any rate, a battalion was drilled there, and the bugle-call of the ancient fortress of Königstein summoned together the best of the youth of East Germany.

What brave, generous men were those first seminarians! After the catastrophe, they heard God singing in their hearts and recklessly followed Him. They had lost their homes, and their families had been scattered like feathers in the wind. Driven away from their villages and towns, they had experienced all the hardships of racial migration. They were turned away from the homelands where their ancestors had lived for centuries, some from the German-language enclaves of Bukowina, some from remote Bessarabia, from Bachka, from Rumania or Bulgaria or the steppes of Hungary, from Silesia, Ermland, Pomerania or the Sudetenland. Some may have survived the death-march from East Prussia or perhaps passed through the bloody Stations of the Cross in the Yugoslav and Czech camps, but most had returned from the bitter years of captivity as prisoners of war, without a chance of seeing their lost homes again and without knowing what had become of their families. Forlorn young men among the sixteen million that had gone under in the storm of Potsdam.

These and the young boys who had risked their lives to escape from the Soviet zone, three hundred and fifty seminarians in all, formed in those days the population of the old fortress. They trained for their mission to souls; they studied, prayed, worked and prepared for the priesthood. They would be the priests of tomorrow. They, themselves, had made their seminary habitable by making their own wooden chairs and tables and toiling, stripped to the waist in the burning sun, to build their own chapel. They were fools, blessed fools, to have come. They had no books, no clothes, no food, no money. They possessed nothing but the flame of their vocation, which they kept burning through all the storms of their adventurous youth. From Tunis to Stalingrad, from Norway to Italy, God had tested them. And now at long last they were able to exchange the heavy tread of their soldiers' boots for the sombre staccato of their own voices praying in the chapel: *Introibo ad altare Dei.* . . .

Here in Königstein, God moulded his hero priests. As exiles they shared the fate of the wandering flock that was to be delivered into their care, the sixteen million that, due to the Potsdam Agreement, were driven empty-handed from their towns and villages by the victorious allies, dishonoured, violated, ill-treated and humiliated to the dust; human rubble from the ruined cities. These were the gentle priests who understood the multitudes that had been forced to dwell in bunkers and barrack camps, where God's Ten Commandments could be obeyed only with heroism. Priests of the poor, who were to give not only their health and their lives, but also their undivided love, to their downtrodden fellow-sufferers, and who were to volunteer for the hardest labour in the Soviet zone and the diaspora. They were to teach their flock to abandon revenge; and to bring the German people to understand that in the interests of peace not all wrongs may be righted here on earth, and that it is sometimes wiser to renounce a strict accounting and to wait for eternal recompense in Heaven.

PLATE 5. The Bacon Priest and his representative in Königstein, Father Coenen, take children from the Frankfurt bunkers and refugee camps to Flanders for a welcome change.

Yes, the glory of the primitive Church lay over Königstein during those early years. Theologians in uniform, their priestly garments were the cast-off battledress of three or four different armies. Their daily rations consisted of two plates of soup with a couple of slices of black bread in the morning and in the evening. There were no books, no study materials, no furniture or utensils. The sheets and the threadbare blankets came from the German field hospitals set up towards the end of the war. A small group of East Prussian nuns, the decimated remnant of a congregation deported to Russia, looked after the domestic arrangements quite miraculously. Seven professors, learned men from East German universities, taught the sacred sciences without any scientific resources.

There was also a junior seminary. In the first class there were forty-five children aged from twelve to fifteen. The fathers of fourteen of them had died in battle or had been reported missing; those of eleven others had been deported to Siberia. Seven of them told me that their mothers had been carried off by the Russians. Two of them had seen their mothers die of exhaustion along the road to exile. Nineteen had completely lost contact with their families. Forty-five children with forty-five different tragedies.

Among the ex-soldiers, Friedrich had been freed from Soviet captivity because of illness. He weighed seven stone (ninety-eight pounds). In 1937 he had begun to study theology. After that he spent six years in the army and three years as a prisoner of war. In the meantime, his family had been driven out of Silesia. He had already learned the addresses of four of his brothers and sisters:

they lived in three different places in the Soviet zone. He had still no news of his parents. His legs were swollen, but he hoped by the summer holidays to be strong enough to earn his living as a bricklayer.

Alfons had been in the navy. During his imprisonment after the war he had served on a minesweeper in the North Sea. After that, he had worked as a farm labourer for two years and had searched in vain for his family— forced to leave the Sudetenland. He had matriculated and had just begun philosophy at Königstein. In the holidays he earned his living as a miner in the Ruhr, and during the school year he gave slide-shows on Sunday evenings about painting and architecture in the Sudetenland.

Joachim had flown with the night fighters and had been shot down three times. He received the Knight's Cross and escaped from a French prison camp. It had been difficult for him to get used to seminary life again. After a fortnight he had been expelled for "insolence". In Königstein things went better. During the Easter holiday of 1948 he walked two hundred and fifty miles from village to village giving performances with a home-made puppet show. His father was severely disabled. He had lost a sister during the flight from Breslau (Wroclaw), and the rest of his family lived scattered about the Russian zone.

Gunthur was from East Prussia. He had been with the Luftwaffe and was taken prisoner by Tito's troops and was well acquainted with all their atrocities. His mother had starved to death during the deportation. All his brothers were killed or missing. His father had died long ago.

This was the human material from which God forged His priests at Königstein in those first years after the war. Aid to the Church in Need has done a great deal for them. Most of this first generation went as volunteers to the Soviet zone, where they live as unknown heroes—unless indeed they are already dead. They were the new type of priest, too few in number, alas, and too quickly forgotten. If only their number could have been multiplied by a thousand, they might have saved the post-war Church.

Königstein also became a "Home for Displaced German Priests". They received help and support from this institution: a shirt, a breviary, money or good advice, a cordial letter from a friend, or the address of a good Samaritan willing to help them. Here they saw the last glimpse of their lost homeland. All this was very important to them, as these elderly priests, together with the six million displaced Catholics left behind after the deportation, had been squeezed, deliberately it seemed, into the wholly Protestant areas of Germany. They had no churches, no tabernacles, no organised pastoral care. Each priest was allotted an average of thirty villages and communities. On Sundays they celebrated Mass as often as five times. They travelled from village to village in all weathers, and often without any means of transport, to baptise, instruct and console. And yet, most of the displaced Catholics could not receive the sacraments on their deathbeds because the priest could not reach them in time.

These priests were underfed and exhausted. Their whole world had fallen in ruins about their heads, and they were powerless to do anything but listen to the tales of woe. For years they cast about for new words and arguments to keep alive the faith of the afflicted Christians. But, as for practical help, they had nothing to give: neither dwelling, blanket, shirt nor even bread and butter. Their preaching of the faith was a voice crying in the wilderness, and their most heartfelt words ran aground on the rocks of poverty. The burden of their apostolate was heavy beyond human endurance.

Priests in rags! They had been driven with their flocks from eighteen dioceses: from Russia, Rumania, Bulgaria, Hungary, Yugoslavia, Czechoslovakia, Poland, Silesia, East Prussia and the Baltic States, all purged of Germans as the starvation columns trudged to the rubble heaps of the West and to the parched steppes of alien lands. There were six thousand of them when this hell broke loose—and only three thousand were left when ACN came to their rescue.

These three thousand priests lived and slept in the attics and cellars of the Protestant population. There they kept the Blessed Sacrament and celebrated Holy Mass. There they heard confessions and received callers, and from there they set out on their rounds. Three hundred of these elderly priests were over seventy years old. More than half of them were over fifty, and only a few dozen of them were under thirty.

Here are some statistics from those days. A Sudetenland priest aged sixty-one served twenty-seven villages and travelled fifteen hundred miles *on foot* in six months. A Silesian priest aged sixty-four served thirty-one villages in a mountainous district, celebrated four Masses every Sunday and walked more than seventy miles a week. In those days there were priests in the diocese of Berlin who had the sole care of seventy or eighty parishes.

It is easy to understand how refreshing the atmosphere of silence in Königstein was to these men, during the summer months when the seminary was empty. For the seminarians, during the holidays, worked on farms or in factories, as unskilled labourers or in demolition gangs, in the Recovery Programme or in the mines. Their seminary counted on this for its maintenance. The only people in the empty barracks were a few professors, the East Prussian nuns and the secretaries for the Register of Priests—the so-called "*Priesterreferat*". This was the time for retreats and conferences for the priest exiles, the weary shepherds of God's wandering sheep. Relieved for a few days by the foreign priests borrowed from Aid to the Church in Need, they could at last escape from the misery, could take a short leave to recuperate in the atmosphere of recollection and affection in Königstein. Here they could pour out all the troubles of their poor human hearts into the sympathetic and understanding ears of their fellow priests.

From the very beginning they came from all points of the compass—from the desolate diaspora regions of Protestant Schleswig and Saxony, from the rubble plains of the West, from the huge bunker colonies of the great cities and even clandestinely from the terror of the Soviet zone. They were a motley crew. They had no cassocks and often no black clothes. They were thin, emaciated. Some wore open-necked shirts, others parts of American uniforms or the old Sunday best of the grandfather of some kind benefactor. Some wore caps or yellow straw hats, others went bareheaded. Many were recognisable only by their Roman collar and a little piece of black cloth under their jackets. Others were totally unrecognisable as priests—weary proletarians in the picked-up rags of the bitterest poverty. There were men disabled in the war, with walking-sticks and artificial legs. There were uprooted scholars who felt their homesickness worse than ever during these brief meetings, reminiscing about their old lives and fingering their old books and papers with trembling hands.

There were some young men among them, who talked passionately about the deep distress of their people, refusing for themselves all financial security, wanting neither future nor shelter so long as their dispersed flocks were deprived of the warm stable of home.

How brave and noble these discussions were! I shall never forget them as long as I live. One felt in these men an ardent love of souls. Their superhuman strength was admirable in its beauty. It was the strength of those who put their trust in God alone. I still think nostalgically of those wandering priests of Königstein. Rejected of men, ignored by the world press, denied by Christendom, but the elect and chosen of God. All the time that I was in their midst, they never thought once of themselves. Their unadorned accounts, the tales of their experiences, the marks of suffering on their martyred bodies, their complaints, their demands—all these things accumulated into a terrible testimony, a crushing accusation against our times, against our contemporaries, against ourselves.

The heroism I discovered in Königstein greatly influenced the further development of Aid to the Church in Need. For years this was the spiritual hub of our activity. The addresses of the itinerant priests adopted by our Flemish children were obtained from Königstein. All but the very first "Distressed Church" congresses were held in Königstein. The distribution of our "vehicles for God" was organised in Königstein. The headquarters of our chapel-truck mission is still in Königstein, and until 1969 the big garage was under the *Haus de Begegnung*— the Meeting House.

The heart and soul of Königstein was Bishop Kindermann, the man whose stubborn and impetuous faith in God created the establishments at Königstein. He was the providential figure who, at the risk of his own life, nourished the bodies and souls of thousands of people in the Czech concentration camps and saved them from despair and death. And when the first refugee bishop, Maximilian Kaller, died of starvation and misery in Königstein, and dozens of seminarians physically collapsed, it was he who hammered on the gates of Rome and on the conscience of the world until God rewarded his faith with ACN.

ACN has, over the years, poured tons of theological books, blankets, clothes and food and millions in financial support into Königstein: and in return we received, by personal contact with its spiritual needs, nearly all the ideas that influenced the development of ACN. As the distress gradually subsided and the exiles in Germany began to feel more at home, Königstein could not possibly continue to have the significance it originally had for ACN. This "home for exiles" was created as a result of problems that have now for the greater part been resolved. As the tide ebbed, so we had to alter our course. From the moment when the centre of gravity of our movement shifted to refugees of other nationalities and to the persecuted Church behind the Iron Curtain, Königstein ceased to be the banner and headquarters of our action. But we look back with joy and gratitude to the heartfelt collaboration of those days, and the stubborn, pious, aged, but ever-youthful Bishop Kindermann and I remained close friends until his death in 1974.

AN INFLAMMATORY IDEA

Time and again I interrupted my begging trips through Flanders for a trip to Germany, so as to come into personal contact with the misery which reigned there. For days on end I drove furiously along the German *autobahns*. Whitewashed cottages and romantic castles dotted the hillsides. But after ten or twenty fertile slopes and the very last green field, there loomed up once more the grey skeletons of the dead cities: Aachen, Düren, Cologne, Mainz, Frankfurt, Kassel, Hanover, Hamburg, Bremen—it was the same everywhere. In places made sacred by the beauty of their cathedrals, the horrors of destruction seemed to tarnish the glory of God.

Horrifying, these parched deserts of stone; horrifying, too, the grey, desolate bunkhouses squatting row upon row behind ramshackle fences, concealing millions of innocent people condemned to a living death.

In my indignation I sent up alarm signals:

It is Passiontide! O Mother, you who wept under the Cross, open the blind eyes of Christendom that they may see the countless sorrowing mothers with dead children in their arms, who were not even granted the time to lay their darlings to rest in the earth by the roadside. Rouse our stony hearts to action, on behalf of the millions of our fellow-men who succumbed here under the weight of the Cross—Men of Sorrows delivered to the

41

hangmen by Christian nations. Let our hearts feel troubled by the camps scattered in such numbers behind the woods and the hilltops or on the edges of the ruined cities. Four families of outcasts dwell together in each of these corrugated iron sheds that have erupted like sores and plague-spots on the infected skin of the earth. See—here between a hut and a torn blanket stands the emaciated horse with which an East Prussian peasant fled to the West. It stands there idle, just as its master sits idle in a dark corner of the hut. He has sold his last possessions and his food ration to buy oats for his horse, the last thing from home that remains to him and his last chance of beginning again if he ever returns. The bleak wind whips the beast's bony flanks. Some morning it will be found dead on the ground. Its master will not survive it long.

Let our hearts be troubled and distressed on account of Salzgitter, a city without a face and without a soul. A city struck dead halfway in its recovery—hideous as a thing deformed, stunted in its growth. A hundred and twenty thousand displaced persons were thrown together here. Members of every tribe and nation, as at the first Pentecost—only the Holy Spirit is absent. The spectre of unemployment haunts every hovel. Fervently and passionately, Catholics pray the prayers prescribed by the bishop of Hildesheim to avert the disaster of dismantling, for if the factories are dismantled, unemployment will double. But the demolition gang continues its work day after day until the future of a hundred and twenty thousand desperate men is reduced to rubble.

Let us visit the transit camp of Uelzen, near Lüneburg, where the refugees from the Soviet zone are received and sifted—a narrow sluice through which an endless stream of people flows. It is the sluice of despair. Thousands of refugees a day succeed in crossing the border at the cost of superhuman sacrifice and hardship.[1] At least two hundred and fifty of them are squeezed through the sluice of Uelzen every day. One million two hundred thousand have already passed through. Gangsters and outlaws, spies and escaped convicts, raped women and those fleeing from the Terror, and many, many children fill the brown barracks. Only twenty percent of them—those whose lives are in danger in the Soviet zone—are allowed to stay in the West; the others are given a railway ticket and a little food to go back with. For they *cannot* be allowed to stay. This unending stream of refugees hinders and disrupts every attempt at recovery: indeed, there is simply no room for these masses of people in a country where half of the dwellings have been destroyed and where the population has been increased by more than twelve million East Germans.

No houses, no work, no food and no money. It is suicide to admit these hordes of despairing people. Yet is it not also murder to send them back? The camp leader raises his hands helplessly. There is no solution, only the clash of contradictions. Send them back? Leave them to their fate? God only knows.

But that is all so impersonal—a matter of statistics. Come with me into these stinking bunkhouses with their four tiers of beds, one above the other. Let us speak to the people. What about this girl? Friedhilde is her name. For four years she worked in the mines of Siberia. Then at last she was allowed to return home, packed with six hundred other girl-slaves like animals into cattle-trucks. She suffers from a weak heart and is bloated from malnutrition. Thousands of others perished in Siberia—she was one of the lucky ones. She found her mother in a

---

[1] This exodus continued until 1961, when the Iron Curtain sealed the border.

bunker at Magdenburg in the Soviet zone. There was even room for her: fifty or fifty-one does not make much difference in the dark. But she was afraid. Of course she was afraid. She was in a state of terror that left her no peace—she had experienced too much among the Russians. So she fled, blindly, to the West. A wild race for freedom from town to town, then the plunge over the border by night. Thence to Uelzen. Here in Uelzen are a handful of officials, a doctor, the British intelligence service and a Commission. Yesterday she was given a ticket to return because West Germany is unable to feed and shelter all these people. So back again, Friedhilde! I talked to her for a whole hour, but I could not convince her. The next morning Friedhilde was dead. She had slashed her wrists. Suicide out of despair.

Dear God! What is to become of all these people? Everywhere sombre, suspicious faces. A lonely, miserable child on a grey rucksack. Mothers with infants in arms. Downtrodden boys from a concentration camp. Children everywhere. Round the camp prowl wild young women, mere girls, with challenging looks and shameless gestures. How could it be otherwise? This bottomless sorrow cries out for just a little numbing, a little intoxication. This hell of Uelzen, this sluice of despair. . . .

This was the situation during the first years of ACN. I implored my people five times, ten times a day; I shouted the truth in their faces; I confronted my listeners with hard facts. I hammered into them that the Communist rulers needed this chaos in Germany, in order to unleash the revolution. That was why, at Potsdam, these millions, with one stroke of the pen, had to be deprived of all their possessions and all their human rights. This was why they had to be dehumanised and degraded in these monstrous camps. They had to be reduced to one thing only—to material from which to make a battering-ram to smash the rest of the world to pieces.

Thus it was that I saw my work for ACN as an attempt to frustrate this Communist plan with spiritual and charitable assistance: to rescue the Church in the borders between West and East—to make Christianity so attractive that it would be acceptable even to the people of the East. A conversation with a Soviet general confirmed me in this view. It took place in Berlin in 1949: the meeting, which was secret, was arranged by a mutual friend. He spoke German well, and we argued for hours. When he went, he said: "We are the select troops of Satan. Are you the best that God can produce?" Are we indeed God's select troops? If we are not the best that God can muster, it makes no sense to speak of a Christian Europe, nor will we possess the strength to fulfil our Christian duty.

We must be God's shock-troops. We must enliven our Christianity with love so that it will be acceptable to others, so that we can pass it on to the peoples of the East, who are soon to take our places in ruling and governing this earth.

This was the great idea, thrilling and simple enough to appeal to all. It put the details of our relief work in a new light, raising it up from the level of welfare movements and placing it at the service of a higher ideal, personally applicable to everyone and easily understood by all.

We have performed a masterpiece of diplomacy in reconciling Christ with the world, in falsifying His way of life, which should be the standard for every Christian, and in adapting His ineluctable demands to our human weakness. His Light does indeed shine in the darkness, but where is the John who bears witness to the Light with living deeds? Europe is not eternal. A world is breaking up, and the centre of gravity has already shifted. Economically and by sheer force of numbers, the future belongs to the East. There is only one task remaining to us—not a political or military task but a Christian, spiritual duty. It is certainly not the task of a Christian people to try to destroy the vital and essentially sound peoples of the East at the very last moment by atom bombs or contraceptives or opium or "firewater" as Christians of earlier times have, alas, attempted to do. Our duty is—to baptise the East!

Without doubt this is the fondest wish of God, before Whom all peoples are equal, that we should pass the heritage entrusted to us on to those who come after us. This heritage is not European culture, or the high perfection of modern "technology", but the Gospel, the Church and the sacraments. We must save for the future the best and most valuable things that we possess—the endless riches of faith and grace. Our Christianity must be as ardent and as shining as a city built on a hilltop or a light on a lampstand, so that others may be convinced that we possess the Truth and the Life!

What is therefore most alarming about our situation, and the most serious weakness of the Church, is the decay of the Christian spirit among all of us: we who should make Christianity acceptable and desirable to the people of future generations, instead of compromising it, as we so often do. We must return to Christ. The only thing that can save us in our extremity is to meet Him face to face. Was it His will to become poor, violated and in dire necessity among the millions of persecuted fugitives so that we should be *compelled* to meet Him everywhere? Could *that* be the reason why millions have had to bear their cross through Europe, so that only the wilfully malicious could refuse Him the compassion of a Veronica and the aid of a Simon of Cyrene? Yes, perhaps our Lord allowed innumerable people in the world of today to become poor and outcast, so that we should meet Him in them and be forced, through love, to cover up the multitude of our sins, so that our Christian lives shine with the glory of the Only Begotten—for love alone will make our Christianity acceptable to those races of the future for whom we are responsible.

This apostolic ideal of ACN was what I tried to impart to the Building Companions. It explains the enthusiasm with which it was received by the people who are still Christians, and especially by young people, who went through fire and water for our Organisation from the very beginning. Even in such places where established institutions and ecclesiastical authorities were at first sceptical, distrustful, even hostile towards the unexpected way in which our Organisation grew, it was eventually the unmistakable fruits of heroic love, the renewal of the Christian spirit and the many vocations that enabled ACN to emerge victorious from all its difficulties.

THE SCHOOL OF LOVE

The chairman of the German branch of *Caritas* once wrote that ACN had taken upon itself, with great success, to train people in compassion. It does indeed seem true that many people have turned into Good Samaritans through contact with ACN, caring with heroic self-denial for the wounds of enemies and strangers.

So we may say that our Organisation benefits not only the persecuted refugee Christians from the East but—far more—the nations of the West. Countless people have discovered and learned the essence of Christianity in ACN as in a school of love.

Because at first our ministry was for the benefit of Germans, we found ourselves obliged in Flanders and the Netherlands to overcome the hatred against Germans and to restore love. Time and time again, in sermons and lectures, I told the story of what happened to me in Vinkt-an-der-Leie.

In 1940 the invading Germans had shot eighty-five men in the village, including the curate. All the old men in the Charity Institute had been murdered. The oldest victim was eighty-nine, the youngest thirteen. There was no family without its victims.

The parish priest of Vinkt was anxious, because ten years after this massacre, hatred was still smouldering in the hearts of his parishioners. He knew that God could not bless hatred, and he put everything he had into up-rooting it, but in vain. At the end of his tether, he asked

me to come one Sunday evening to talk in Vinkt
about the poverty and distress among the Germans. I
must admit I was pretty scared. I went to Vinkt the
day before to reconnoitre. I arrived at the priest's
house on Saturday evening. The priest raised his arms
despairingly.

"It's hopeless, Father. The people here won't tolerate
it. They're saying: 'Is he actually coming to ask for help
for the Germans? For those devils that shot our men and
boys? Not on your life! He can preach as much as he
likes to empty chairs. And he can thank his lucky stars
he's a priest or he'd be in real trouble!'"

What was I to do? After consultation with the parish
priest, I decided to prepare the way for the evening
meeting by preaching first at all the Sunday Masses.
The next morning I surprised the parishioners by ap-
pearing in the pulpit and preaching on love for a whole
quarter of an hour. It was the most difficult sermon I
ever preached in my life, and it was a success: for when
I was saying my thanksgiving after the Mass, when the
church was quite empty—people are ashamed of showing how good they are!—a woman came shyly up to
me. She said nothing, but gave me a thousand francs
and was gone before I could say anything. Fortunately,
the priest was just coming out of the sacristy and saw
her leave. He told me she was a simple farmer's wife.
Her husband, her son and her brother had been shot by
the Germans in 1940. She was the first.

During the course of the day the parish priest took
me to various meetings with youth groups in preparation
for the evening lecture. He also took me to visit the
most sorely bereaved families so that I could explain my

ideas in the family circle. We prayed together for the success of my enterprise.

In the evening I had a full hall. I spoke for two hours on the "rucksack priests" and the abandoned Catholics. I did not ask for bacon, for money or for clothes. I only begged for love. And at the very end I asked if we could all pray together for our brothers in distress in Germany.

They prayed with tears in their eyes. Later, at about eleven o'clock—when it was dark and nobody could see them—they came one by one to the presbytery to hand in envelopes with 100 francs, 500 francs, maybe a letter added as well. And early the next morning, before I left, they were again at the priest's door.

I received seventeen envelopes full of money. They paid money into our bank account. They collected bacon. They adopted a priest. That was Vinkt!

The school of love! Among my papers I find the account of an incident at the Holy Sepulchre School in Turnhout, where the children have generously been sending parcels to fifty Iron Curtain priests.

One of the nuns writes:

It was the first morning of the school year. Shining faces and freshly starched pinafores, all sparkling with good-will and ready for a fresh start. The fourth commercial form is all present. Everyone has something to say about the holidays. A girl comes along with a message.

"Agnes, the head mistress wants you."

Agnes, as is usual under such circumstances, makes a quick examination of conscience and climbs the blue steps hesitatingly but curious, followed by nineteen pairs of curious eyes. Then she returns, a newspaper cutting in her hand, and bursts out:

"Our Iron Curtain priest is dead."

A shocked silence falls on the lively little group. Some younger children standing about look up from their chatter in surprise. What could so unexpectedly have stopped their noise? The news goes round the playground like wildfire:

"Have you heard? The fourth commercial's priest has died. The Head Sister has just told them."

A small girl of the second form glances anxiously at the Head Mistress to see if she has anything to say to *her*.

In the meantime, Agnes, helped by the other nineteen girls, is translating the German report. They already know all the facts in the short biography of the priest from his letters; indeed, he had told them many more details. But the sober words of praise threw a fresh light on some of those things known to them from the four-years' correspondence. When she comes to the short sentence saying that he remained on the "most cordial terms" with his parishioners from behind the Curtain, Agnes says quietly: "*Wie es daheim war, ist es nimmer mehr*" (It will never, ever be the same as it was at home). Dear Agnes! She learnt that by heart and still remembers it from the first letter, when she knew no German.

"I should like to read those letters again: after all, we were only twelve years old, four years ago. Shall we ask the Head Mistress?"

There are thirty of 'those letters'. Next Thursday, they all meet to reread the letters from their Iron Curtain priest with all the love and understanding of which girls of sixteen are capable. The letters revive many small forgotten details of their own school life.

"Don't you remember, Marie-Louise, how afraid you were that our priest might have to go hungry if we didn't send anything during the holidays?"

"And how much we argued about what he would like best when were sending our first parcel!"

"Yes, there were five of us in the shop, and it took us three quarters of an hour to make up our minds."

"And what about the time when we didn't pack the coffee in the middle of the parcel, and there was only an empty bag when it arrived!"

"Look, his handwriting is getting more difficult to read."

"He must have been ill already."

"He was always so glad to get our letters."

"And here is his last letter, dated June 22, 1953. That's just seven weeks before his death. He was still hard at work."

There was a silence for a few moments, and then:

"Do you think the medicine I got for the last parcel arrived too late? And perhaps it wasn't the right kind anyway—we didn't know what he was suffering from."

But Agnes comforts her by saying:

"The medicine's bound to have done other people good. He always used to say in every letter that the best thing about them was the love with which everything was sent. He said that what they needed most was love."

With sudden understanding they reread how pleased he had been with their parcels, especially because the nutmeg, tapioca, sugar and all the rest were packed in brightly coloured paper tied up with ribbons: it showed how they had put their whole heart into it. . . . Then they take up his last letter, much shorter than the others but showing so plainly what a hard, lonely life their Iron Curtain priest had lived:

"The bishop has been here to administer Confirmation and there was a lot to prepare. As you know we are only a small community here, and there were only sixty candidates for Confirmation, so the bishop stayed only three hours. Everything went off very well, and he was very pleased. Of course, there were quite a lot of problems with the preparations, but fortunately I was able to overcome them, and my health held out, too, thank God. My warmest thanks for the parcel, which was again a great joy and came in very handy for the bishop's visit. . . . May the Holy Spirit help you all in your examinations at the end of the year. I shall pray for you. I also ask for your prayers, and remain, very cordially and gratefully, Yours . . ."

They stayed together for a while in silence. In their sorrow, they understood a little of how much they owed to him, their Iron Curtain priest. They were grateful for his prayers and his example, but especially because, by living in misery and poverty, he had taught their young hearts to love and to appreciate something of the great human needs of the times.

The next day they all went to the Mass they were having celebrated for the "repose of the soul of our priest."

"But he will certainly be in heaven!"

"Then for everything he asked us to pray for when he was alive!"

Their Iron Curtain priest was sixty-two.

I have been running through his letters and have stopped at his last short message. I can read between the

lines how poor and lonely he was, how desolate and
forlorn in that small village among strangers who were
not his own people, and under the jurisdiction of a bishop
who was not his own bishop. He was no longer in good
health, which made his burden twice as heavy. But in
none of his letters do I read that he had lost heart, though
it struck me that he had to fight hard to keep his courage.
And in every letter, like a moving refrain: "*Es ist alles
gut*" (All is well).

There is so much suffering hidden behind the sober
story of all his troubles, great and small, as he told them
plainly and simply to those few girls in Flanders—"his
class", his dear helpers.

Hidden beneath the sorrow of these children of fifteen
and sixteen there is evidence of a growth towards higher
and better things. This is what our girls owe to ACN:
the ability to care for others—and those others, almost
strangers—with selfless love; the ability to learn what a
woman can do best: to give . . . to give everything, to
give of herself to alleviate bottomless misery.

The school of love. The Netherlands also had their
share in it. The people there are said to be more busi-
nesslike and calculating than the people of Flanders, and,
rightly or wrongly, it is sometimes thought that the
Dutchman counts his profits even in love and does not
easily lose his head. But Kees Griffioen, who travelled
through the whole of the Netherlands with the "St.
Martin's Truck" for ACN, can tell another story. This
is the touching story he once told me of a new coat:

> Most mothers follow fashion from afar. By means of
> new buttons, an altered collar or a new clasp, a ladies'

PLATE 6. A heavy load for the helpers in Aid to the Church in Need's warehouse, in Antwerp.

winter coat can be made to last for quite a few years. But the moment comes when there is nothing more one can do about it.

Then even the most self-sacrificing mother suddenly gets the feeling that she really looks a sight. And there is certain to be a friend of hers who will ask whether she has had three or perhaps four years' wear out of the coat. This is the question that causes mothers, who are always willing to spend money on their husbands and children but seldom on themselves, suddenly to begin saving very secretly. They need a new coat—at all costs.

The savings box waxes and wanes with her generosity. When she starts paying more attention than usual to fashion books, and when she walks back to a shop window she has already looked at, it is a sign that the time has come. . . .

Once one of these mothers had the good fortune—dare to call it anything else!—of having a visit from the ACN St. Martin's Truck to her parish the day before she was to buy the new coat. She heard of refugee mothers and their children in the camps suffering from the cold at night because they had no blankets, no woollen clothes, nothing to wrap their babies in. She heard of mothers whose children were fatherless, because the father had been arrested or deported, or simply disappeared. Some fathers had abandoned their families; others were only a memory, an unknown Russian soldier—a devil incarnate. She heard of mothers obliged to work as factory hands, who had to leave the care of their little ones to strangers.

A good mother does not live only for her children. She always has some bond with other mothers, no matter what class, nationality or race they may be. All mothers have the same joys, the same sorrows, the same anxieties.

All mothers think first of their child and of children. The mother who needed the new coat could not get all this out of her mind. She *had* to do something for another mother.

Then she did something heroic. She did it anonymously, but the deed was repeated many times. She gave away the only thing she had been saving for so long. Not the old coat that she would not need when she had the new one, but the money she had set aside for the new coat.

Later on, when her friend asks her if she has had the coat for four years, or is it five, there will be a smile on the face of that mother. She will think of the garment that for all eternity will suffer neither from moth nor from fashion, because it is worn by a brother who has Christ within him.

The school of love. One Sunday I had preached seven times in a church in Coblenz. After the eighth sermon, during the evening Mass, I went round myself to collect for ACN. Afterward I found an envelope in the basket, containing the ignition key of a Volkswagen and a letter. The letter read as follows:

Reverend Father, I heard your sermon this morning; I came back because my conscience will not give me any peace. My father is wealthy and gave me a Volkswagen for me to enjoy myself. I don't think I can keep it any longer. Give it to a priest behind the Iron Curtain. Enclosed you will find the key. The car is parked in front of the church with the license plate number KO. . . . All the documents are in the glove compartment. Don't try to contact me: the left hand need not know what the right hand is doing. Just pray that God may grant me the grace to become a priest. . . .

In Switzerland I went preaching with my chapel-truck through the Canton of Schwyz. The collections were very generous. In one small village a young fellow came racing after the chapel-truck as we drove away, and threw a fat envelope into the collection box. I discovered afterwards that it contained ten thousand Swiss francs and the following letter:

> This is my inheritance. It was given to me because I am going to get married in three months' time. We need the money, but you can do more good with it behind the Iron Curtain. I have discussed the matter with my fiancée and she quite agrees. We have made this sacrifice so that God may grant us the strength to approach the altar on our wedding day with pure hearts.

In Antwerp I once had to speak at a meeting that was attended by six hundred working-class women. I had been allotted a speaking time of ten minutes, and I talked for twenty minutes. The lady who chaired the meeting, a very distinguished lady, was getting nervous; but I just carried on talking and didn't stop. When I had finished, a woman shouted: "Let's have a collection." The lady in charge said: "Not now, first we have other speakers." But two or three other women protested: "No, Father should have his collection now; he has to strike while the iron is hot." Then I thought to myself: this is the moment! I took the lady's hat, a hat with a little feather—it was a very nice hat—and I said: "I will take the collection myself, and if two or three others would like to help me, we'll be finished in five minutes." And I was off right away. We did finish within five minutes. I received forty thousand francs—three hundred pounds!—from six hundred working-class women. The little feather was broken, it is true, but I had the forty thousand francs.

Once, I was in Wiesbaden, Germany, at St. Boniface's Church, on a weekday evening. I had drawn seven hundred people into the church. I preached, and then after the sermon I placed myself with my "Hat of Millions" right there at the door. Many people had not known that there would be a collection, so I told them: "If you have no money with you, or not enough money, you can come as late as two o'clock tomorrow afternoon. You can put your donations through the letterbox of the presbytery, in an envelope 'for the Bacon Priest'. Then you can bring the large notes, which you probably haven't brought along now." Although I explained all this in the church at Wiesbaden, many people wanted to drop their contributions into the famous "Hat of Millions", and so a man in the first row acted as money lender—people borrowed money from him so that they could give their donations right then and there. I collected four thousand marks from seven hundred people, and also five gold rings (two gold wedding rings among them), a gold watch, two pairs of ladies' gloves, a pair of nylon stockings—new stockings, of course—and afterwards a man came to me in the sacristy and said: "One moment, please, Father." Then he pulled off his sweater and handed it to me for the poor refugees from the East.

In 1958 I had four hundred chalices made out of the gold and silver people had donated. An old widow came to me, a refugee woman, and she told me: "Father, I am poor and I don't have any money to spare. But I can give this. This belonged to my husband, who was killed as a soldier in 1915 during the First World War. I have always worn this ring, but now I'll give it to you for a chalice for a priest behind the Iron Curtain."

In Munich: "I enclose two rings belonging to my husband, who was killed in action. The wedding ring has been cut because the hand of my husband had stiffened in the cruel cold. I make this sacrifice for my three children, especially for the two boys, so that the Lord may help them during their studies and, if it is His will, may call them to the altar."

Once, I preached in a small town in Switzerland, and the next day I found in the letterbox of the presbytery an envelope containing 500 francs and this note:

"Dear Father, now you shall have this for the persecuted Church. I have been saving this money for months to buy curtains for our new apartment. Now the old curtains will have to do for a bit longer." Signed: "A mother with four children."

In the Ruhr district in Essen, Germany, I found a wages envelope among the money in my "Hat of Millions": "Friedrich Krupp, Essen. Part payment for the week from the first to the seventh of July." It contained 85 marks in cash. The poor fellow had donated a whole week's pay for the ACN.

In France I received this letter from a Hungarian refugee: "Praised be Jesus Christ. I am a refugee, and once I was as poor as our brothers and sisters in Eastern Europe. I am a lot better off today. I am not rich. I am only a labourer; but I give this to God with all my heart. I pray for His blessing and opportunities for a good job, so that I will be able to do good works more often. With

PLATE 7. Refugees on pilgrimage in Waldürn in 1952. Even the dispossessed give donations for those who are even poorer than they are themselves.

much gratitude. A refugee from Hungary." And a thousand French francs were enclosed with the letter.

In Holland I once preached in a sanatorium, and on the next day I received the following message scribbled on a piece of paper: "You have greatly enriched me by your sermon. Take, as a gesture of gratitude, the 650 guilders enclosed for your relief action. Please, pray for my fiancée and myself, so that, if it is the Lord's will, we may recover our health and be able to marry. Or that He may give us the strength we need to remain chaste and to offer our illness as a sacrifice for the persecuted Church."

In Vienna: "I enclose a hundred schillings for a poor refugee-seminarian as a token of appreciation for my recovery from a serious illness. May God protect you, dear Bacon Priest!"

In Hanover an old refugee came to the presbytery late in the evening after the sermon. He came from Silesia and was seventy-six years old. He brought me two gold coins—20-mark pieces from the time before the First World War. He told me: "Father, I have kept these gold coins ever since 1913: they were a sort of iron ration. I saved them even when we were expelled from our old homeland. I didn't give them to Hitler. But I give them gladly to the Bacon Priest!"

The school of love! Let me proclaim the love that burned like a great fire all over Europe, where the call of ACN moved people's hearts.

Do you recall, you poor widow, telling me how your husband had died in a concentration camp leaving you

PLATE 8. It was in Essen in 1954 that the Bacon Priest obtained one of the best results in the early days of his begging campaign for refugees and the persecuted Church: 190,000 DM in cash, 40 tons of gifts, 4 cars, 47 motorbikes, 6 kilogrammes of gold and silver jewellery and 13 kilogrammes of old silver coins.

with twelve small children? You had tears in your eyes when you explained to me how difficult it was for you not to hate the Germans. . . . Yet it was your desire to contribute the widow's mite, and you wanted so much to be the first!

The school of love. Even the cattle-drover, a master in drinking and swearing, learned his lesson there, when, without hesitation, he sent me five tons of lean horse-meat and an introduction to a canner who, in his turn, turned bacon and horse-meat into a hundred thousand tins of "German sausage", all free of charge. Who, I wonder, in Germany is wearing the Sunday suit of that man who was shot, which his widow gave to ACN with tears in her eyes? And where is the precious cradle of the stillborn girl which was brought to our storeroom by her mother? And where are the shoes that stout-hearted Virginia took from under the bed of her sick parish priest, saying that he would not need them any more as he wouldn't last much longer? And think of the dozens of young people who gave up the money they had saved so hopefully and with such difficulty for a holiday or a pilgrimage to Lourdes or Rome.

What pleased God more—the savings-bank book with 130 marks given by a seventeen-year-old schoolboy or the 800 marks of a German curate who was struck by this example? And think of all the blessings that will rain down from heaven on account of the heroic act of my anonymous friend, an octogenarian living in an attic in Ghent, who chose to be poor for the Church in distress and who sent his whole fortune of a hundred fifty-six thousand francs to ACN.

There are many touching anecdotes. I shall never forget little Fritz in Ulm, who heard me preach in the children's Mass on Sunday, and who wandered for hours through the town the next day with his full moneybox and a sticky bar of chocolate clutched in his little hands, looking for the Bacon Priest, until the police brought him to me with these precious possessions. And the poor elderly nuns in a Dutch convent who, choosing to remain cold, joyfully gave to ACN all the money they had saved to have central heating installed.

Dear God, how splendid it all is! I could write a hundred pages of this kind to prove to you that ACN is a true school of love for all people of good will. People are much better than we imagine. They all seem to be capable of heroism. They are only waiting for a word of fire to set their hearts ablaze. Then Christianity can begin again—the only thing that can save us.

We are a small peninsula in a great continent. We are the small remnant of a spiritually ruined world. We have no duty to ourselves, only a vocation for the future. We ought not try to save anything for ourselves. What we keep, we keep for destruction. What we resign in love belongs to God in any case. And if we ourselves belong to Him, we may yet perhaps be able to overcome the power of darkness: for love is stronger than death!

FROM RUCKSACK TO CHAPEL-TRUCK

It has been of great help to us that our relief was aimed at priests or was sent through the hands of priests to our afflicted fellow-Christians. Thousands of letters from itinerant priests, read by a hundred thousand school children and at least half a million adults, were a guarantee that the whole of Flanders was constantly being reminded of their bitter necessity.

The following are fragments of letters written in those dark days:

> I am living in two attic-rooms measuring ten feet by thirteen feet, in the house of a Protestant family. The first room is my kitchen, parlour, study and bedroom. In the second room I say Holy Mass during the week, on a bookshelf. About six people can attend Mass—maybe ten in a pinch. On Sunday we celebrate Mass in a Protestant church, but the minister does not allow it during the week.

> Scattered over thirty-five Protestant villages and hamlets there are seventeen hundred dispossessed Catholics, whose priest I have been for two years. The pastoral work is hard, often full of bitter disappointments, but also full of pastoral joy. We have seven "schools" where I teach the catechism to one hundred and fifty Catholic children. I celebrate Holy Mass regularly in three of the more centrally-situated villages, where I also teach the young. I live in the loft of a Protestant farmhouse. It also serves as a church and parish hall. On my bed,

three chairs, a small bench, some boxes and planks, I can seat thirty-five to forty children for the catechism lesson. During the week I say Mass here. At first I held choir practice here, because our people are not happy if they cannot sing during Mass, but then the farmer forbade it. Every week I travel thirty miles by bicycle, often in rain and snow, over icy roads and paths, through mud, slush and, in summer, dry sand. I have lost two stone (twenty-eight pounds) in weight since Christmas. But a little slimming is not so bad when you are fifty-nine.

We travelling priests have to do without practically everything. We have no cruets and no ciboria, no bicycle pumps or clean shirts. We need writing paper, and we need a car desperately. And above all, we need something to alleviate the hardship of our sorely afflicted people. But I must not complain. The colleague who is my nearest neighbour is far worse off. He has not even a bicycle and has to walk at least forty miles a week. Moreover, he is sixty-three and greatly troubled by an old wound from World War I. But in spite of this we keep going strong. . . .

In the misery that has befallen our poor people, for most of them the priest is the only piece of home that is left to them. May God help me to keep going for a while longer, and may He soon send help.

If only we had one consecrated place where a person at the end of his resources could take his problems to the Saviour in the Tabernacle! But we are deprived of even this comfort. A small attic, measuring ten feet by ten feet, where I keep my things, where I live and sleep, is my parlour and my presbytery. At the same time it is the chapel where I celebrate Holy Mass at a home-made table. . . .

The work is very hard here and we are all as poor as churchmice. But poverty has brought us the freedom to devote ourselves entirely to the spiritual care of our compatriots. For we are aware that one single sacrifice of the Mass outweighs the wealth of the whole world. But it is heart-rending to think that we ourselves are too poor to give a little earthly bread when sad children ask for it with feverish eyes. Fortunately there is ACN to send us something that we can distribute now and again!

Without such letters we would probably never have succeeded in overcoming the incredible resistance, slander and opposition raised against our Organisation.

Thank God that, during the anti-German fury of the first post-war years, the simple people were still Christian enough to retain their respect for the priesthood. And what a priesthood! For the generation of rucksack priests, which has, alas, almost disappeared on account of the doubtful blessings of the German "economic miracle", was certainly an awe-inspiring phenomenon amid the ruins of Germany.

I went to see these men doing their rounds in their vast parishes on motorcycles or in ancient jalopies, on ramshackle bicycles or on foot. Most of the Catholic displaced persons had been transported to regions of Saxony and Hesse with no Catholic churches and with no pastoral care. There I found refugee priests who were obliged to break their spiritual bread in eighty, ninety and even more villages. Priests in rags and tatters, as poor as tramps: they kept the Blessed Sacrament in their attics in a cigar box or a table drawer, in a ciborium made from an old football cup. They could not genuflect when they passed in front of the "tabernacle" at every other step. They celebrated Mass in classrooms, barns, dancehalls, inns and Protestant churches. It was quite normal for them to say four or five Masses on a Sunday. They worked until they dropped—I did not find it difficult to arouse pity and love for the rucksack priests.

In those days I also preached in Germany, mostly in Protestant churches, not to beg, but to encourage and console, searching for the right word to touch the souls and the hearts of those outcasts. It was the gospel of love from across the border. Often the displaced persons walked fifteen or twenty miles to hear me. They waited patiently for hours, praying their many Rosaries until I arrived with my spark of light in their night of faith. During my clumsy addresses they shed tears of emotion. Their priest, too, would have tears in his eyes.

Then it struck me that foreign priests could fulfil a great mission here as ambassadors of the universal Church. In thirty-five Dutch newspapers I published the following article on the need for priests in the German diaspora:

A room in an inn is not a worthy chapel; the huts and barns are falling down, but God does not consider it beneath His dignity to share this dog's life with the least of His children. He visits His flocks in the ragged garments of the rucksack priests and in the Eucharist. But it is also His will to visit His flock in the person of helpers and Good Samaritans who will make His shape visible to the poorest of the poor and prove His mercy to the least of the Germans. And this is where our task begins. It is we who must visit them in their misery and be their benefactors. We must travel East with relief columns. We must send priests to drive heavily loaded trucks of food and clothing. We must put ourselves at the disposal of the itinerant rucksack priests in the German diaspora, going on their rounds with them from village to village of their immense parishes. We must say Mass, preach—just an encouraging message from their brothers across the border—and distribute with generous hands all the gifts contributed by the love of the Christian West. We must make Christ shine out clearly amidst this black misery. We must make the motherly compassion of the universal Church something tangible to those who for more than five years have been sunk in the dark night of despair.

This article, which appeared in 1949, contained the basic idea of our chapel-truck mission. Five months later the first Dutch "mobile church", consecrated by Cardinal de Jong of Utrecht, rumbled over the German roads. The Dutch Railways supplied, in all, twenty huge trucks. The diocese of Ghent collected the money for fifteen Opel chapel-trucks. Since then, hundreds of priests from seven different countries and dozens of Orders and Congregations have been on the road in their mobile churches, year in, year out: preaching and encouraging, baptising, hearing confessions and distributing Holy Communion—and also giving material gifts to four million of our abandoned brothers in the Faith, reached by this missionary venture in the regions without churches.

The spirit of the universal Church breathed round these chapel-trucks. They were like the Epiphany of a

great, energetically radiating Christianity, filling everyone with admiration and making the hearts of even the
most solitary Catholic outcasts beat with renewed Christian pride. For the chapel-truck mission was the first
great manifestation of the Catholic Church in Protestant
regions since the Reformation—in areas where the
Church, for centuries, had neither face, nor name nor
respect. This encounter, which some years later was
repeated by thousands of Building Companions, removed all kinds of prejudices and fulfilled one of the
conditions without which the *Unam Sanctam* cannot become a palpable reality.

The chapel-truck mission was also a victory of
catholicity over that parochial outlook which even now
has not yet been completely eradicated. In the last century, unheeding Christians allowed their heritage—the
social teaching of the Church—which they had betrayed,
to be taken up by others, mixed with poison, and given
as food to the oppressed. By the time this fact was recognised—*Rerum Novarum* came some forty years after
the *Communist Manifesto*—it was too late. Now another
essential feature of the Church was being fought for: her
catholicity, which, during two world wars, had been forgotten and practically denied. The cry for a larger community, one reaching beyond the contention of states
and nations, has been heard by Freemasons and socialists.
We are in real danger, in spite of the most uncompromising of papal documents, of again forgetting our catholicity through our obsession with *our* people, *our* country,
our diocese and *our* abbey and of again not being able to
read the writing on the wall.

It was an unforgettable experience to see these mobile

churches returning from their hazardous journeys every year. While the engines were still hot and the drivers were polishing up their gigantic vehicles for the final parade, all the missionaries gathered in the conference hall at Königstein to exchange impressions and to review their six-month apostolic journeys.

How impressive the farewell ceremonies were, especially those of the first few years: the music of purring engines, the festive church bells ringing from all the loudspeakers and the Te Deum chanted by thousands of voices as this column for God drove away rejoicing to the battlefields of spiritual conquest.

Through dust and mud, rain and wind they drove to the crumbling front of the universal Church, where the bishops of many dioceses had called for their help. Each mobile church was manned by two missionaries and a sacristan-driver. Where possible, each truck was entrusted to the province of an Order that would see to the regular replacement of the missionaries.

I have before me an enthusiastic report from the year 1953:

> The chapel-truck missionaries, 136 in all, have this year carried the message of God's mercy to more than a thousand villages, where almost 110,000 dispersed Catholics were visited personally by them. With anxious hearts, they discovered how the long years without church or priest had left their mark on these unfortunate people. They found more than eight thousand mixed marriages, five thousand of them invalid. But they fought doggedly for God's heritage in these menaced regions. They appealed to these people in almost seven thousand sermons, and almost seventy percent of those

who could come received the grace of the sacraments in the confessional and on the wooden steps of the altar. With full hands they distributed almost two hundred and fifty tons of gifts, and from these poorest of the poor they were able to collect thirty-five thousand German marks for the training of new refugee priests. . . .

The chapel-truck mission, which until the 1960s was financed by Dutch Catholics, is still the glory of ACN. Even when material distress was overcome in Germany, the spiritual necessities remained greater than ever in those regions where Catholic dispersed persons were moving in ever growing numbers to the industrial areas, leaving a remnant behind to die out gradually. For these last remaining Catholics, churches could not be built. God's wandering shepherds, the nomads of the mobile churches, were often the only ones to care for them at all.

CLOTHING, WHITE DRESSES
AND SWEETS

In those years, we were hammering into the people we spoke to the fact that all nations form one whole and that we are responsible for the others. We have continuously pointed out that the Church has the task of leading the persecuted and the outcasts to Heaven, too, for these unfortunate Christians are our brothers and sisters, and Christ died for them.

Yet these unfortunates were, in those dark years after the war, the pariahs of Christianity. And the only ones who could alleviate their suffering were the wandering priests, who had died in their hundreds because *we* had remained indifferent for too long. The words of these priests were without effect, because the best preaching in the world will founder if it is not supported by works of Christian charity. Although Western Europe still called itself Christian and averred that it had taken up arms to preserve Christian civilisation, that very same Christian Europe, during the first years after the war, allowed the outcast and exiled priests in Germany to die like dogs.

Against this background I made my appeal in 1949 to the women and mothers of Flanders:

> The front line of God's Kingdom runs through Germany. If the hordes overrun the Church there, then there will be no stopping the tide of spiritual devastation.

If we want to save the Church in Europe, we must make ready—whatever the cost—to save the Church in Germany. If we continue to ignore the refugee priests and leave them to their fate, it will be impossible to preach the Gospel to millions plunged into the blackest misery. And we cannot then be surprised if one day these millions rise up and tear down our tabernacles.

We have an obligation to Catholic unity. We must with our whole heart and soul become the consolers and helpers of those whom Christ called "the least of my little ones".

Women of Flanders, you are neither rich nor very prosperous, but your generosity was always great when the Church was in need. Your money, your possessions, your sons and daughters you sacrificed blindly for the Kingdom of God in your own country and abroad. Will it now be said of you that you turned away, indifferent to this crying need in the wounded heart of Europe?

No and no again! Once more you will show that Flanders belongs to Christ, and that love is the supreme law here. You will give us the chance to go to the East with our hands full, so that we can save these priests and, with them, the Church. ACN has begun. Christian charity has already stormed the ramparts of hate and misunderstanding between nations. The spiritual blockade of German Christianity has been broken. Throughout the whole of Flanders the children have already risen, to save first the priests and then their expelled flocks. God has chosen the weak and the despised to confound the strong. Women are also called upon to help in this crusade of charity. ACN relies on *you*.

How can we thank those simple and nameless women for the mercy and the love they showed to German priests and Catholics after this appeal?

Let me give one example. A woman had lost her husband in a German concentration camp. The district Secretary of the Women's Catholic League, going her rounds for ACN, thought she should be tactful and passed over this sorely afflicted widow. But love works miracles: the widow came herself to the Secretary to give her dead husband's last suit—for her, as it were, a relic—for ACN.

The response to the clothing campaign of 1949 was overwhelming. First the post brought piles of letters and postcards—on each postcard, a few lines denoting heroic charity. A collection of messages long and short—taking hours to read—speaking, especially between the lines, of the generosity and pity of the simple donors. Then followed the raids with borrowed trucks on hundreds of parishes and centres where the various women's institutes had piled up their booty. Day-long excursions through all the lanes of Flanders! Triumphant homecomings when the overloaded trucks entered our warehouses.

Next the donations had to be sorted. This task went more quickly than we had thought, because in many places numerous volunteers had given up their spare time, their afternoons and evenings, to lighten the load for us. There was happy astonishment at the extraordinary quality of the goods collected, bearing witness to the motherly hearts of the benefactors who had given the best that they could spare.

Finally the goods had to be pressed and packed into great bales before being transported to Germany, in batches of fifteen tons or more at a time. In long processions of trucks, hundreds of tons of clothing arrived in

Königstein and, in accordance with the lists of requirements sent in from various places, were sent on to the rucksack priests. From these enormous stocks, each priest received what he needed, in the right length and size, both for himself and for the most needy of his exiled Catholics.

After several years of a fruitless apostolate in wildernesses of misery, these itinerant priests at last were able, through the generosity of Catholic Flanders, to support their heroic preaching of the Faith with tangible gifts of Christian charity. At last clothes and shoes were available to alleviate the most pressing needs. At last they could carry in their helping hands the proof that the universal Church lends her ear with love and pity to all defeated and outcast people, even to Germans.

Immediately a wave of gratitude flowed back to the West. The letters arriving in Tongerlo were like the first notes of a song of joy that resounded in ever-growing and mightier harmony over the towns, the villages and the cottages of t'his little country, a country that had suffered much itself in the course of the centuries, but one where hearts had remained warm and generous—a lovable country.

Love should be measureless, boundless. It should be ready not only to provide the bare necessities for brothers in need, but also, after the example of our Heavenly Father, be prepared to give "the rest that shall be added unto you".

For this reason we did not hesitate to say *yes* when we were urgently asked from all parts of the refugee areas in Germany and Austria to supply white dresses for the little girls who were to make their First Holy Communion under such sad circumstances.

At home, in the white and gold baroque churches of the Sudetenland and Silesia, they were used to proud beauty and fervent splendour, and now they were to celebrate this glorious feast in worn-out rags! Was it right that these children, who had never seen a real church, a tabernacle or a confessional, should, through the whole of their youth, learn nothing at all of the glory of our religion? Was it not desirable for their religious future that they should have at least *one* fine memory of their childhood, *one* unstained joy to look back on and to cling to in their later years? Of course it was a mere question of outward appearances: but such things are indispensable for children, whose minds are not yet susceptible to abstract truths and reasoned proofs.

This was why ACN considered it necessary to send to the refugee Christians, through the hands of their priests, not only the bare necessities of life but also the "extras".

Thousands of Catholic mothers in the German refugee areas had cut up the last pieces of material they possessed that seemed suitable for a festive occasion to make the small bridal dress to receive our Lord. One rucksack priest wrote us that he had cut up his curtains to make white dresses for two orphan children, so that they could be as pure as God wanted them to be on that one special day. Then we made an appeal for white dresses for the little brides of our Lord:

> See if you can find a white frock somewhere at home that might suit this purpose (matching shoes and

stockings are welcome, too, of course) so that we can pass it on to the grateful hands of a sorely tried mother who, at the First Holy Communion of her daughter, will look back, as you did, to the bright horizon that was once her life. You fathers and mothers who read this, perhaps you have no little First Communicant this year, but maybe you can find in one of your cupboards a Communion dress, a dress that a little bride of Christ in Germany is waiting for.

Both in the Netherlands and in Belgium the reaction was amazing: ten thousand Communion dresses were generously contributed. With one of them there was the following letter:

"In this box is Hadewych's First Communion dress. She is the eighth of twelve children. She gives it up gladly for the First Communicant of a Catholic refugee family, although it means she loses her place as an angel in the parish procession. Signed for Hadewych by her father."

Some weeks later, for the first time in four hundred years, processions of children in white followed the Blessed Sacrament through the Protestant regions of Germany, and somewhere in Hesse or Schleswig a weary mother shed tears of joy when her Edeltraut, radiant with happiness, made her First Holy Communion—in Hadewych's dress.

Let me now recall the "Sweets Campaign" organised by ACN. It began one Lent. Anneke, Rob, Godelieve and some hundred thousand other small boys and girls had listened silently to the story of little children in camps and behind the Iron Curtain. The boys frowned and a sympathetic sigh from the girls rustled through

PLATE 9. A "sweet" campaign. Flemish children make up bags of sweets for Easter and First Communion celebrations for the German diaspora.

the class at the climax of the story. And somewhere in Flanders two tears stole from the heavenly blue eyes of Maryke, when Sister with her gentle voice told about little Hedwig, Hedwig the refugee-child who was given a holy picture by the Bacon Priest. And when the priest had said that Hedwig must hang this picture up on the wall at home, Hedwig had answered, "We haven't got a wall."

Yes, these stories told by schoolmasters and mistresses were the reason why so many thousand flaxen or dark-brown heads nodded their consent when asked to make a little sacrifice during Lent for those unfortunate children.

This was the start of the ACN Sweets Campaign: seven weeks of mortification for the sake of the poor. Please do not underestimate it! A great deal of love and self-sacrifice was needed, not to speak of generosity, childlike heroism and self-restraint, to pile up sixty tons of caramels, chocolate, boiled sweets, peppermints, biscuits, nougat, pear-drops, toffees and other delights into mountains of sweetness! With the varied fortunes of war, a great battle was waged for the bar of chocolate from which a small boy's teeth had bitten off three tiny corners before generosity prevailed, and the large piece that still remained was dropped into the box provided. And how precious in God's eyes were the tears that little girl shed when she brought her largest and most coveted Easter egg to the Sister to give to a little refugee. The convents and schools and the Tongerlo warehouse were buzzing with activity during the Easter holidays, with all the volunteer helpers patiently and deftly sorting, weighing, packing, adding greetings and children's addresses and decorating the parcels with colored ribbons. Then for weeks the heavy trucks of ACN thundered across Europe to the central distribution warehouses and to hundreds of refugee camps, barracks, ruined castles and bleak settlements where children from all the countries of the East were spending a joyless youth, and experiencing, often, the tortures of hell.

Again a month later I found on my desk one of the many letters in response, from the Wrangel barracks at Rendsburg. There, in the soldiers' empty rooms, the almost bestial life of hundreds of adults was shared by 153 children—their names were written on a long list attached to the letter of thanks. A hundred and fifty-three children, doomed every night to observe unspeakable scenes. Children, of whom Christ once said in indignation: "Whoever shall offend one of these little ones, it were better for him that a millstone were tied around his neck and that he were drowned in the depths of the sea."

Here are the exotic names of those children: Viola Zalkovski, Marita Hazala, Nina Poroch, Lyla and Tereza Styrcs, Helle, Kalwe and Sulew Ots, Stoja Peskyte, Ute, Lothar, Marion and Traute Mischke, Merija, Erika, Rolf, Werner and Helga Kühl. Their names are registered with the administration authorities of Rendsburg, just as they are registered in God's Book of Life. Against each name has been carefully entered how many packets of sweets Karin, Hannelore, Tatjana or Mykhailo has received. But God has also written, after each name, how many millstones are necessary to avenge the ruined souls of Anita, Indra, Borys and Harald. The Rendsburg official writes to thank us for the short pleasure given to Ilze,

PLATE 10. Even the helper who sorted the shoes received words of praise and encouragement from the Bacon Priest.

Dace and Zane. But God will curse us if we abuse the sacrifice of our children to lull our own consciences to sleep.

For with this Lenten sacrifice of the children a chain reaction began that we cannot now bring to a halt. Here are the links of the chain: Godelieve, Anneke and Rob have done their best to help Waltraut, Velga, Siegrun and Lorelies in the hell of the Wrangel barracks, and awakened a glimpse of joy in the precocious eyes of Klaus Grochowina. And the joy of 153 East European refugee children awakened a human feeling of gratitude in the heart of an official in a dusty administration office. And this gratitude inspired the letter with the 153 children's names. Now God throws back this letter onto the dismayed consciences of—you and me.

What will happen next? The letter is waiting for an answer. Not an answer from our children, but action from us. Let our children offer their sweets: we must do more. We must open our hearts and purses and set to work feverishly, pray passionately, love selflessly and search unremittingly for ways and means to relieve the distress and solve the problems. Then, and only then, when we have done everything that our utmost efforts can do, will God Himself intervene and liberate this world. For in such measure as we show mercy God too will show mercy, rebuild the ruins made by men and make the future once more livable and sunny for Godelieve, Tatjana, Rob and Karin, and for all the children of this earth.

"VEHICLES FOR GOD"

In the early years of ACN, when our work was still centred on the German refugees, we not only built chapel-trucks, but strove even more to increase the effectiveness of the itinerant priests by motorisation. This was at the end of 1950.

Then, in one week, three rucksack priests died in Germany.

The first was thirty-nine years old. One evening, after his sixth Holy Mass, his motorcycle collided with a tree—he was so tired that he could not keep his eyes open. He was killed instantly.

The second was forty-one years old, and he served thirty-two villages on foot. He had a fatal heart attack.

The third was forty-six years old. Three priests in one week.

The day after this tragic news I was in Bremen visiting a rucksack priest there. This man had fifty-seven villages and a bicycle. He had ruined his health in three years. One evening, after his fifth Mass and a forty-mile ride through the rain, he collapsed at the altar. He was taken to a hospital in Bremen, and he was lying there when I visited him. The doctor had told me beforehand that he had at the most two months to live. He was courageous and smiling. But suddenly he had tears in his eyes when he said to me:

"Father, do you know what the worst thing is? When I add up the balance of these years in which I have offered up my young life, I can see that eighty percent of my people died without the last sacraments. Not because they did not ask for them—they were longing for them— but because I had only one body and just a bicycle."

I went back to Tongerlo and begged my friend Albert Kuyle to plan a campaign to supply at least a hundred priests with Volkswagens. All the press and especially the young had to be mobilised for this purpose. It became one of the most successful campaigns of ACN, procuring a hundred twenty Volkswagens in the first two months. Then the enterprise was continued, in aid of non-German refugee priests and of the persecuted Church behind the Iron Curtain. Since then our Organisation has made many thousands of cars and motorcycles available for the Church in need. But never to be forgotten, for those who experienced it, is the beginning of this campaign and the radiant day in March when the first thirty cars were distributed in Germany.

Vercammen was at the wheel, racing yet again down the *autobahn* in the service of ACN. In the Chevrolet sat Canon Dubois, a Belgian parish priest, and myself. It was Monday, 3rd March. Yesterday a Volkswagen from Roeselaere had preceded us. Tonight four irrepressible representatives of the West Flanders Catholic Students Action will follow us.

Cologne, Düsseldorf, Dortmund, Bielefeld, Hanover: Vercammen passes them all. The needle of the speedometer swings between sixty-five and eighty miles an hour. The Chevrolet purrs like a contented animal.

PLATE 11. A rucksack priest on a visit to one of the many diaspora villages. Before, he had to go on foot or by bicycle to care for them.

The silver ribbon of the *autobahn* stretches out straight through the country and makes a slight curve past the rumbling factories of the Ruhr and winds playfully through the Teutoburger Forest and the Weser hills. We are travelling towards Hildesheim, where the first thirty Vehicles for God, presented by the good people of West Flanders, are to be blessed and distributed tomorrow.

We reach Hildesheim in the evening: the ruined heart of a diocese larger than Belgium. It was reduced to rubble on 22nd March 1945, but in the middle of the ruins the famous thousand-year-old rose bush still grows and blooms in season, just as the courage and the energy of bishop and priests remain unbroken. The sound of bells calls the faithful to the Church of St. Godehard for Benediction and my sermon on the theme of Flanders' charity. Then the emotion aroused by a singing congregation such as one can find only in Germany, followed by my collection in the church porch with the hat that had gathered millions.

The 4th of March. At eight o'clock a car, grey with dust, stopped in front of the House of Charity. Four weary, laughing fellows in the blue uniform of the Catholic Students' Action alighted. Refusing to take no for an answer, they had crossed Belgium twice yesterday to get their passports and visas sorted out, and driven all night to be here in time. This is the way we do things in West Flanders and ACN. Canon Dubois smiled approvingly at his men.

At the Pontifical High Mass, two thousand people crowded between the pillars. German hymns echoing in the vaulted roof. Festive music, the cathedral chapter in purple, Canons in violet robes and sparkling pectoral crosses, and our Canon from Roeselaere in a borrowed cassock among them. My sermon was on the "Vehicles for God," and how the newspapers and the youths of Flanders had made it possible to motorise the front line of the universal Church with a hundred and twenty cars.

Then came the blessing ceremony. The people streamed out of the church singing. In a great square formation stood God's vehicles, decorated with wreaths of evergreen and white flowers and bright flags. On the front of each car was the emblem with the words "Ost-priesterhilfe Flandern". Inside was a "shield of origin", giving the year and name of the donor. Thirty green, shining cars—a brigade of brotherly love—and thirty gloriously happy priests. Most were old and tired, but there were also one or two younger soldiers of God.

Cope and mitre glinting in the sun, the bishop walked round the cars blessing them. Thousands of people thronged into the square and over the ruins; with a full and solemn sound, the hymn "A House of Glory" echoed over the old city. Then the Canon delivered an address, first in German and then in Flemish.

Next the names of priests who were to receive a car were read out. They were from the four North German dioceses of Hildesheim, Osnabrück, Münster and Pader-born. They had travelled a day and a half to get here. These were strange names: Father Kalabis, Paul Krafczyk, Kurt Nowak, Peter Slawik, Hugo Jendrzejzyck, Otto Jarits, Karl Szmanda and many others. They had come from a long way, from regions where Germans and Slavs had lived side by side for a thousand years, sometimes fought, and especially had enriched each other.

Then the second series of names echoed over the mul-titude: Bruges, Nieuwpoort, Poperinge, Bavikhove,

PLATES 12/13. Twenty chapel-trucks from the Netherlands setting off for their first mission amongst the German diaspora.

Courtrai, Waregem, Izegen, Ypres and many others, all names from World War I, which may well be the reason why the Germans were so deeply moved. Twice thirty names—the roll-call of want and the parade of love: the heart of the Church encompasses the whole world. After that, a word of thanks from a rucksack priest, and from the bishop, and then from many thousands of throats the hymn *"Grosser Gott wir loben Dich"*. Photos were taken, and then followed the lunch at which there was so much to be said that there was hardly time to eat anything. The bishop presented me with a splendid gilt Bernward cross, and an old abbey near Bremen was offered for me to establish a Norbertine monastery among the displaced Germans. The four fair-haired boys from Catholic Students' Action were sent to bed by the Canon, and then the return home in the gently purring Chevrolet. A woman threw a handful of snow-drops into the car. Vercammen at the wheel, radiating virtue and contentment, watched the speedometer vary between sixty-five and seventy-five, while Flanders raced towards us through the twilight.

So ended the first stage of the "Vehicles for God" campaign. A month later, seventy cars were distributed in Königstein, and then another thirty. Even now not a week passes without ACN gladdening the heart of some weary refugee-chaplain in Australia, Scandinavia, France, Belgium, Germany, England, Spain, Italy, Austria or South America with a car—something without which he cannot possibly fulfil his mission. And far behind the Iron Curtain, bishops and priests drive the Vehicles for God that they owe to ACN.

GRAIN FOR CHURCHES

We shall now tell of the tragic and marvellous experiences of Johannes Hruschka, a chaplain in Götzenhain, a town in Hesse. It is 12 June, 1949, Trinity Sunday and a special youth day. The only place available to Father Hruschka is a room at an inn, for which he has to pay the exorbitant price of 50 marks. Yet he would like to have something special in his wretched "church" for his celebration. He has received a donation from an American Army chaplain. He knows how well disposed the foreign chaplain is towards his miserable flock, but having observed the well-nourished figure with his ever-present Lucky Strike cigarette, he feels that "this man does not realise the extent of our misery".

Father Hruschka invites the American chaplain to attend the evening ceremony: the chaplain accepts. At the appointed time Father Hruschka hears the noise of the jeep outside his window. The two priests walk towards the meeting-hall of the inn, the one carrying the Blessed Sacrament, which he has just taken out of his wardrobe, the other silent and bareheaded. In the distance they hear the murmur of many voices. Why don't the people go in? Is the hall not ready? The parishioners have gathered from three villages, four hundred hot and discouraged people. A protest rises from the crowd as they see their pastor approaching: "He won't let us in!" Father Hruschka's hands clasp the pyx with the Blessed Sacrament even tighter. He is filled with a cold dismay: God is not allowed to enter. Vaguely he notices how the chaplain beside him stiffens with disbelief. He sees his people, the disturbance, the indignation and the closed door. But he feels God upon his breast. His hand beckons the hesitating crowd to remain together and he hears himself say: "Wait! It'll be all right!"

Father Hruschka tries to persuade the landlord gently. He appeals to his honour. He pleads passionately for the God he carries with him. Five minutes, ten minutes, a quarter of an hour; it seems an eternity. In the meantime, the Army chaplain stands near the door, and from outside he can hear angry cries and half threats. At last the landlord gives in and reluctantly opens the hall to the people.

Father Hruschka is trembling all over. The good-hearted American understands his condition and takes over his duties. In spite of everything, his heavy voice creates a devotional atmosphere in the crowded hall. Beside his improvised altar Johannes Hruschka kneels with his head in his hands, praying a prayer without words from the depths of his humiliated, priestly heart.

In September the owner finally closes the doors of his inn to the Catholics. His excuses are so many that everyone feels he has none. God then finds new accommodations: the gymnasium and dance hall belonging to the local sports club. New Year's Eve approaches. The Catholic community of Götzenhain has gathered well-disposed to receive God's blessing on the coming year. Their priest addresses them. He is one with them in their hardships as refugees, and this common fate is a consolation and balm to their wounds. But hardly have the last parishioners left the hall when Father Hruschka, together with the sacristan and altar boys, has to begin clearing up as quickly as they can because the *Einheimischen*, the "locals" of the place, are giving a dance to-night.

New Year's morning. At five o'clock parish priest and sacristan are back again. It is a revolting business, trying to coax the last lurching figures to leave the hall; they talk drunken nonsense and try to embrace the priest and the sacristan. After this disgusting scene the windows are thrown open to allow the cold morning air to cleanse away at least the stench of cigarettes and beer before God re-enters. Both men wash the floor and with great difficulty clear away the filth of the night's orgy. As they start once again to set up the altar, the sacristan breaks out in a fit of bitter discouragement: "This is just a pigsty! Here we are, working for days to get together some altar linen and a couple of candles and all we've got is a stable where I don't know what has been going on all night. Give it up, Father. This is no work for human beings. What good is it to God if we can't give him anything better than this filth?"

He stops when he sees Father Hruschka's white face and weary eyes. The priest is silent. This is the worst blow, that his poor attempts are not appreciated even by his own people, who know what it has cost him to get as far as he has. It seems almost blasphemy to celebrate Mass now. He cannot even keep his thoughts together at the altar; the whole time that nerve-racking jazz and the hopeless words of his assistant re-echo in his ears. What must God think of this licentious place? . . .

The New Year passes in trouble and care. The Holy Year 1950, a year of great expectations and great disappointments, is for the Catholics of Götzenhain a year of superhuman perseverance.

Christmas again. Father Hruschka wishes to have a midnight Mass for his people at the end of this difficult Holy Year, even if it must still be celebrated in the dance hall. They have worked and sacrificed the whole year for their new church, and until it is built—he dares not say how inadequate the funds are—he must do what he can to make up for what they are lacking.

With a few assistants he has set up the Christmas altar, and between a couple of fir trees the Child of Peace stretches out His arms over Götzenhain. Everything looks nice and homey. The parishioners are present in such numbers that they have to stand up against the altar and behind the manger. His work in the bitter cold has not been in vain. *Memento Domine* . . . Remember, O Lord, Your scattered flock in Götzenhain, look down on their trust and their perseverance and remain with them. Among all that they have lost, the lack of Your presence bears hardest upon them. God of Mercy, do not forsake us.

High Mass with the same atmosphere, the same disposition. Now to clear up; all the decorations they put up with such care must be taken down again—there is going to be a meeting of the Athletics Club.

Boxing Day, December 26, very early. Priest and sacristan put everything out again as well as they can. Sung Mass; then pack everything up again; there is a ball this evening.

Sunday, New Year's Eve, the same thing again.

New Year's Day. Despite all their efforts, the decorations are now grubby and dingy. Father Hruschka feels, too, that the Christmas atmosphere has gone. The shepherd is worried about his sheep, about those who have forgotten the way to the dance hall—and about the others who are persevering (for how long?) with the support he is able to give them, which seems so hopelessly inadequate. In spite of all his trouble and good will, there will be no improvement so long as he has to call God down from Heaven to a place like this.

Knowing all this, Father Hruschka, when Christmas was over, turned to us with a request. During these days of deeper peace—or greater misery—God sent this priest to us. He was one of the hundreds standing in the breach, a living witness to the superhuman effort with which those helpless and defeated people fought for God. God's hand lay on the priest, the hand that once for all eternity had written down the great commandment: "that you love one another as I love you."

This is what Father Hruschka wrote:

> Our refugees can take two roads: either they succumb, under pressure of their years of affliction, to godless extremism, or they will preserve the faith of their fathers, in which case they will be purified by suffering; they will atone for the faults of their people and of others. But in the latter case we must provide them with the means to build new Catholic churches, the indispensable focus of all religious life. They will become one of two things: either dynamite or valuable building stones for the extension of God's Kingdom.

> We have done our utmost, but things are still extremely rudimentary. A number of Protestant churches

are available to us, but there are many places where the Lord has to make do with an inn or a dance hall. That is how things are in Götzenhain. Our people do not feel at home in such places, and many neglect their religious duties on this account. They cannot readjust. They have lost the homeland of every Catholic—their church!

Hence this urgent prayer to our Catholic brethren in Flanders, who still have the benefit of having churches of their own. Help us to complete our church. Our community, which consists almost exclusively of refugees, has collected—at the cost of much self-denial—the sum of ten thousand German marks. But without help we cannot complete the work. Help us to keep and to win back the souls redeemed by Christ's blood.

We assure you we shall be grateful. Every Sunday the clergy of Götzenhain will pray for the intentions of all the benefactors who have helped to build God's house, and God will bless their self-denial. For the sake of immortal souls, please help us!

> Johannes Hruschka,
> Pastor of Götzenhain,
> nr. Offenbach/Main, Hesse.

This cry for help, and many other letters in which we were asked urgently for help to build churches in the diaspora, forced us at last to start a new project: "Give the Lord a Handful of Grain". This was to provide us with the necessary means to build a number of refugee churches or at least to help to finance them. The country girls of Holland and Belgium visited all the farms in their neighbourhoods with paper bags printed with the Aid to the Church in Need emblem—strong paper bags which would not tear easily. Some days later they would be collected by young peasants with carts and be delivered full to bursting point to the local warehouse of the Farmers' League, which would organise the sale. The money obtained was for us.

Millions were contributed, and we were able to finance the building of churches in the refugee areas. Johannes Hruschka at Götzenhain got his church, and so did Josef Artel in Gambach, and others. The example of the peasants was infectious. Students at Utrecht University started a campaign and built a church for Josef Schneider at Freiensteinau, and everywhere in Holland and Belgium money was collected for some refugee priest to help him build his church. A year later our Belgian department began recruiting volunteers, who would speed up the building of churches throughout Germany by working without pay. These were the precursors of the Building Companions, whose members, financed by ACN, lent their backs to the construction of dozens of new churches for the displaced Catholics. With gratitude towards our many benefactors, we can now say that the regions along the Iron Curtain, which were once entirely Protestant, are dotted with hundreds of little churches, which ACN helped to build with love and enthusiasm.

GOD'S FORTRESSES

Great was our delight when, on 24th September 1952, Bishop Kerkhofs of Liège wrote a pastoral letter calling on his whole diocese to help in the new task that Aid to the Church in Need had set itself: to build a line of spiritual fortifications along the Iron Curtain.

The bishop's decision was surely inspired by the awareness that the East can only be reconquered for Christ if the Church in Germany remains strong and active; and that in the de-Christianised parts, where the fate of the Church in Europe will probably be decided, there is more need of spiritual powerhouses than military bases.

So it was that the Bishop of Liège decided to build a "fortress for God" in the German diocese of Fulda, as proof of living solidarity with those brothers in Christ fighting on the borders of the Kingdom of God. It was to become a focal point of prayer and apostolic zeal, a monastery with a retreat house and accommodation for all outcasts, refugees and destitute people, for whom the gift of a piece of bread will often decide whether they will curse or bless God's name. The house was to become a spiritual centre for the lonely priests serving their many villages for sixty miles around, and who are the only shepherds of tens of thousands of refugee Catholics. It was to be a point of departure for religious from Holland and Belgium who were assigned the duty of relieving these priests in their superhuman labours. Foreign volunteers, too, would be welcomed to help bear the burden of their German confrères in the neighbourhood of the monastery. This is how the significance and task of the monastery of Berbra, God's first stronghold in front of the Iron Curtain, were described in our sermons and press releases back in 1952.

All this had been carefully planned. Aid to the Church in Need had already set up a research institute at Königstein, whose main task was to draw up a scientifically-prepared plan for a series of centres in the German refugee areas. We did not want to work "blind". Our work would extend over many years, and had to be founded on a solid basis.

The institute's first job was to prepare a demographic map of the German diaspora. Accurate statistics were compiled as to the number of Catholic refugees, their districts of origin, their professions, their families, their possibilities for the future, their religious practice. These data were compared with the industrialisation plans and the agricultural and development programmes of the German government. On the basis of this comparison, our sociology experts were able to determine in which districts the refugees would remain. It could be predicted at once that the refugees would leave those areas where no industries were being established. This gave us prior knowledge of how various regions would develop from an economic point of view and what the population graph would look like over the next few years. These were the data upon which Aid to the Church in Need developed its plans.

It was on this imaginary but reliable map of the future that the plans for the fortresses were drawn up—thus

PLATE 14. Königstein in April 1951. Cardinal Frings gives his blessing to the foreign and German chapel-truck missionaries at the "launching" ceremony.

avoiding the danger of bad investment. For we had in mind the example of churches built without an eye to the future, which had become superfluous after a few years because the Catholic population had moved elsewhere.

The basic plan comprised the rebuilding or setting up of monasteries at Celle, Brunswick, Hanover, Kiel, Salzgitter, Bebra, Hof, Stuttgart and other places.

Heroic sacrifices were made for the realisation of this plan. The diocese of Liège collected eight million francs for Bebra, where not only a Capuchin monastery, but also a nuns' convent with a dressmaking school, hospital and kindergarten, was built. Our benefactors in Holland financed a Redemptorist monastery in the Salzgitter district, the greatest achievement of the whole grand enterprise. Ireland helped to build a Dominican house in Brunswick. The diocese of Bruges created a stronghold at Celle, on the Lüneburg Heath. The Building Companions built a tower of prayer, a contemplative convent of Poor Clares, in the neighbourhood of Hanover. The Netherlands branch of Aid to the Church in Need financed a Slovakian convent near Salzburg.

At the dedication of Bebra, Bishop Kerkhofs, with tears in his eyes, expressed his hopes: "May this base become a home where itinerant priests can receive warmth and strength. May it become a sanctuary where the benefits of divine mercy and goodness are called down upon the outcast. May it become a stronghold of God, radiating the light of consolation and renewing strength. May it become the living symbol of true love, uniting men without discrimination. May it carry forth the gospel of peace and love that the Redeemer brought to mankind. May it become a worthy successor to those bases founded in these same regions by the great missionaries a thousand years ago. May it be the first of a whole series of Fortresses for God, forming a chain of love of which Bebra is the first link."

Immeasurable blessings have rained down on the Catholics of the diaspora through these monasteries. Could this perhaps be the reason why our plan met with such great resistance, and why such enormous sacrifices were required before the first monasteries could be built?

I feel I owe it, as a debt of gratitude, to call to mind the sacrifice of Godelieve Rommens, who at the age of nineteen laid down her life as the spiritual foundation stone of the convent of Celle. It was the building of this convent that cost us the greatest exertion and the bitterest struggle of all.

It happened in Roeselaere on 14th March 1954. That Sunday, our preachers had made an appeal in all the churches on behalf of the convent at Celle. I myself spoke in the Patria Hall that same evening. That Sunday evening, not ninety hours before her death, God gently asked a great sacrifice of an ordinary girl, a sacrifice for the heavily disputed convent at Celle, and for the forlorn souls He had been willing to entrust to Aid to the Church in Need.

It has been our experience that people are much better than we think, that many are just waiting for a great ideal in order to abandon themselves to it without restriction, that a great many are quite prepared to lose their heads and allow their hearts, and grace, to speak. This is how it was with Godelieve. Ninety hours before her death she listened to God and looked for something to sacrifice, something that would hurt a little, as I had asked in my address. And she did find something. She had been saving for a long time for a journey to Lourdes with her twin sister. Supposing she gave these savings to Aid to the Church in Need? That would certainly hurt. Her eyes were wet for a moment when she told her mother of her decision in the evening. But she put on a brave face and acted as if those few thousand francs were only a small thing to her. And she didn't say another word about them. The other girls, whom she was helping by the chapel-truck, noticed nothing. She was happy and cheerful and playful . . . and also a little reckless, by nature. She worked like a horse, lugging parcels and armfuls of clothes about. She had a kind word and a smile for everybody who entrusted his gift for Celle to her. She didn't feel herself the least bit a heroine on account of her money-box. She was just plain Godelieve Rommens, laughing and romping in her usual way.

Only God saw her differently, because He was struck by her magnanimity. In His great love He must have thought that her pure soul was *now* at its finest. No, dear God, we cannot blame You for picking Your flowers when they are at their best, nor for wanting to embrace Your dearest children first. That is why You took Godelieve to You, ninety hours after her great decision.

There was dismay and cries of woe round her bleeding body lying in the street. There was mourning and sadness in Roeselaere. There was—as hardly ever before—sincere sympathy with the sorrow of father and mother and of the whole family, who were able to bear this heavy cross with Christian resignation and almost with pride.

Let the world call her sudden death under the ACN chapel-truck a tragic accident. But it was not so in reality. For Our Lady of Flanders, St. Godelieve and her Guardian Angel took little Godelieve to God's throne with smiling faces. For those who die for love will be crowned by God's love.

We buried her a few days later. The sun struck flashes of glory from the processional cross. The girls sang those joyful hymns of the liturgy of the dead. ACN was present with the finest wreath we could find. There were long lines of priests and thousands of people who prayed and wept tears of emotion. A simple Flemish lass, crowned princess by grace and by her great love, went on her triumphant progress through Roeselaere on her bridal journey to Jesus.

The campaign in Roeselaere was a success. The good people were very generous. But more valuable than the tons of foodstuffs and greater than the enormous sum of money was the pure sacrifice of Godelieve Rommens. Far away in Celle, near the Iron Curtain, where the stronghold for God has since been built, this sacrifice bears fruit. In gratitude and in pious memory of Godelieve Rommens, Aid to the Church in Need has dedicated an altar there to St. Godelieve, the saint from Flanders.

Two years later the monastery was consecrated. Sun and storm-clouds gave the ceremony a character of its own. The bishop of Bruges had arrived by airplane in Hanover the day before; a crowded coach filled with guests of honour from West Flanders had started on its way at five o'clock in the morning; private cars from Roeselaere and Tongerlo brought others. It was an

PLATE 15. Cardinal Frings and Father Werenfried in 1954 inspecting one of the fifteen new chapel-trucks donated by the Flemish diocese of Ghent.

PLATE 16. Holy Mass at the chapel-truck for Catholic refugees in a Protestant village.

unbelievable collection of people: there were young
Building Companions with their chaplains, the Catholic
Students' Action in their blue shirts and yellow ties, the
episcopal master of ceremonies, the episcopal deputy for
ACN with his staff of priests and lay helpers; Remi and
Piet, who had organised the chapel-truck campaign
throughout the diocese; publicity workers from our
headquarters at Tongerlo; and those quiet workers for
God—elderly mothers, shy maiden ladies, sturdy fel-
lows—who, at the Bishop's special request, just *had* to
be there to see the crowning of so many years' sacrifice.
And who else was there? The father and mother of
Godelieve Rommens, together with the indefatigable
Staf Vermeulen in his position as member of the Execu-
tive Board of Aid to the Church in Need—and myself.

We had all rallied round our bishop, seventy-two
Flemings with flags and hymns, carrying the images of
our Lady of Dadizele and of St. Godelieve, with chalice
and ciborium and an armful of vestments, which were
to be laid as an offering, immediately on arrival, on the
marble top of the altar of the Lord.

As the times of unilateral help for Germany were already past, the Women's Institute of Hildesheim, which
had contributed the German share of the expenses of the
new church, was also present. There were forty Bar-
nardo boys from Berlin who were escorting their guardian, a Dominican prior, to the spiritual fortress of which
he had been appointed commander—only he was to die
some months later, as a result of the inhuman demands
of his apostolate—and thousands of people from Celle,
refugees from the East who would find here a home for

their souls. Priests, too, had streamed in from near and far, together with the imposing purple-clad Administrator who, after the death of the old bishop, represented the grateful Christians of Hildesheim.

At seven o'clock on Sunday morning the solemn consecration of the church began. The creamy white building gleams tall and slender in the morning sun. A fresh wind snatches at the bunting as the tall figure of the bishop of Bruges approaches the church—a soldier for God, a man who in spite of his heavy task in his own country could still take to heart the necessities and cares of the Church in danger, abroad.

He brings the ancient Latin texts to life with an unexpected stress and intonation, a glance or a gesture to underline the words. A heavy gust of wind from the blue and white sky is the response to his first invocation to the Holy Spirit. The choir of Dominican friars, with black cloaks over their white habits, sings the ancient psalms and canticles.

This Fortress for God was built in spite of everyone and everything. I myself had to threaten to return my German decoration to force the sale of a piece of land. Time and again the plan was sabotaged; we were refused a building permit. Then the men of West Flanders lost their patience. Young fellows from all the colleges of the diocese borrowed an ancient bus and drove to Celle, with fists clenched. Unannounced, they stood there with nothing but faith and their young muscles. It became a spontaneous endeavour. They knelt in prayer, made a big sign of the cross and began to dig—without a permit. They dug like madmen and laid the foundations all in

PLATE 17. An impressive sight. The parade ground of the barracks in Königstein is used to park the chapel-trucks and "vehicles for God" during the "launching" ceremony.

PLATE 18. Cardinal Frings blessing the first seventy "vehicles for God" provided by Flemish students and youth groups for the rucksack priests.

one go. Never did people work so hard, and the letters we received were unlike any we received after any work. This intrepid band of students, by the *fait accompli* of the foundations, made the first breach in the barricade of wickedness and misunderstanding, that barrier against which Aid to the Church in Need had to fight constantly. And now the bishop of these fighting youths is driving out the last devils from the sanctuary built upon those foundations.

The procession crowds into the church. A thrill of emotion passes through the multitude when the locally unfamiliar names of St. Charles the Good and St. Godelieve are read in the litanies—these are the Flemish saints whose relics, together with those of St. Hedwig of East Germany, are sealed into the altars of this church. The altar is being consecrated, and an old bricklayer watches with amazement as the bishop, with an unmistakably professional touch, flourishes the trowel and closes up the tomb of the relics. Suddenly fire springs up from the altar in five places. Flames leap up, and dark clouds of smoke rise, with the "*Veni Sancte Spiritus*" to Heaven.

The church consecration takes almost three hours. During the interval before Holy Mass, the bishop consecrates the images of St. Godelieve and Our Lady of Dadizele.

Entranced, the Germans listen to the flood of hymns that flows on for almost an hour, until the bishop returns for the first Holy Mass to be celebrated in this church, packed to overflowing. At the altar stand priests from Flanders, hard-working men who feel more at home in the pulpit, in a chapel-truck, at a mass meeting or in a building camp than officiating in a complicated pontifical service. That is how I feel, too, next to the episcopal throne. But with three masters of ceremony and a bishop who smiles patiently, even when I put his mitre on his head back to front, all difficulties are overcome. And in spite of all the cares and worries of the masters of ceremony, this High Mass will remain unforgettable for all those who were able to attend it, inspiring gratitude and joy and a steadfast will to fight on for the Kingdom of God—which is the sole aim of Aid to the Church in Need.

One of our finest achievements was certainly the convent of Herrnau in Salzburg, built by the Dutch Catholics for a congregation of nuns driven out of Slovakia. As God's Providence played such a manifest part in this affair, I cannot refrain from giving a short account of the foundation of this convent.

It began in the year 1937 in Czechoslovakia. Ten women full of apostolic fervour joined in profound union with the Sacrifice of the Lord in the most Holy Eucharist, to do penance and to assist priests actively in their pastoral care. The country was torn asunder by hatred and nationalism. The movement to set up a national church was like a crack in the structure of the Church. The salt of the earth had lost its savour. Tepidness and indifference destroyed in many their appreciation of the sacraments. The new religious community, founded by the zealous Bishop Gross of Litoměřice, was to be a stronghold against the threatened de-Christianisation of the country.

After nights of terror and darkness, a handful of these helpless nuns found themselves one fine morning in Salzburg, destitute and homeless, like children of Providence.

PLATE 19. A "Fortress for God": the Redemptorist monastery of Steterburg in Salzgitter-Thiede, one of the twelve headquarters built by Aid to the Church in Need to provide special pastoral care in the refugee areas.

Even now the Lord chooses the small and weak for the realisation of His plans. For eleven years they lived in a narrow alley behind sunless, damp walls. Sickness and death were their companions in this un-hygienic dwelling. But in spite of the dark, little rooms, the flame of love burned bright in their hearts, so that more and more new girls joined the outcast religious in their dark house. The community began to grown in its hidden life.

The nuns in grey seized courageously at every opportunity to assist as home help, nurse, parish secretary, social worker or catechist in the work for refugees and the Church in distress. But no form of active life could make them forget the charge they had received from Bishop Gross and from their prema-turely deceased foundress, Mother Maria Chotek: to become rescuing angels for the unfortunate country that had rejected them.

A sermon on ACN and a folder explaining our work for the Church of silence brought the congrega-tion that was struggling for existence into contact with our work. After discussing the matter with them I gradually came to the conclusion that these Sisters of the most Holy Eucharist, with their apostolic inter-est in the East, would responded perfectly to the programme and ideals of Aid to the Church in Need. And it also became clear that this community would only be able to fulfil their important task if they could develop in normal conditions and accommodation. This led to the decision that a Fortress for God would be built in Salzburg, one of the spiritual key points between Lübeck and Trieste, where, in the words of the Holy Father, preparations were to be made for peace.

It was summer 1957 when we took this decision, and it seemed impossible to burden the already heavily overstretched budget of Aid to the Church in Need with the expense of building a convent. On the other hand there was no time to waste. I advised the nuns to take out a loan, and promised to stand guarantee for the payment of one year's interest. In 1958 we would pay off the loan with the proceeds of the campaign in Salzburg and pay for the rest of the building: thus we could begin a year earlier with the foundations of the convent.

As the nuns were unable to give any security for their loan, every bank refused to advance the money. My promise that Aid to the Church in Need would redeem the loan next year, did not appear safe enough for any banker. It seemed that the plan would have to be postponed; but, moved by the tears and supplications of the good nuns, I found a solution at the very last moment. I took out a life insurance policy for the amount of two hundred thousand German marks, to be paid if I should die before the end of 1958—payment was to be made to the German *Caritas*. Then I took the insurance policy to the Chairman of *Caritas* and asked him for a loan of two hundred thousand German marks for Salzburg. My argument was as follows: "If I die you will get the money back from the insurance company; and if I don't die I can keep on preaching, and you get the money back from Aid to the Church in Need. So there isn't the slightest risk except in the case of a nuclear war, and in that event it doesn't matter who loses the money."

The Chairman smiled and pleaded for my proposition with the Board. A week later I received the money I had asked for, and the building of the convent began at once.

The Dutch section of ACN took upon itself the repayment of the loan and the responsibility for all further expenses. Dutch Catholics gave enthusiastically for this bulwark to the East. In 1958 the nuns moved into their new convent—together with postulants from various countries who, after my sermons and lectures, had volunteered for Salzburg to prepare for a better future for Slovakia.

In the Herrnau convent in Salzburg, young women from Czechoslovakia, Austria, South Tyrol, Switzerland, Flanders and Germany are learning the Slovakian language with diligence and love. They are being specially trained for pastoral care and welfare work. They are receiving this spiritual and ascetic training so that they may become—now in Austria, and later on in the East—valuable and devoted assistants of the priests. In their simple chapel they pray for Aid to the Church in Need, for the persecuted Church and for their beloved Slovakia.

This new stronghold for God built by ACN was not, this time, for priests but for a modern congregation of women prepared to go to the East with prayers and service. There, more than ten thousand nuns were assassinated or perished in forced labour camps and prisons; millions of our brothers in the Faith are waiting for the helping hand of strong, pious women dedicated to God. It was *our* duty to create the possibility and the material means to fulfil it, so that these brethren need not yearn in vain. And it would be a sorry scandal, indeed, if the girls of our times did not prize or respond to the Cross, and to the splendour of a religious vocation lived for the glory of God and the salvation of souls.

So we built twelve monasteries and convents. In keeping with the great traditions of evangelisation in olden times, we did not think it right to limit ourselves to building churches, training new priests and sending out chapel-trucks. Help could be most swiftly brought by building monasteries in each new ecclesiastical district; for there was a real danger that so much time would be lost in organising *normal* pastoral care that there would be no souls left to care for by the time this perfect system of churches and chapels was at last completed. The Church had no time to lose, and the finest church building programme would be worthless if in the meantime the falling away of the refugee Catholics could not be stopped by effective interim measures.

The monastic houses founded by ACN, explicitly praised by His Holiness the Pope, had the task of bringing immediate help in those areas where the organisation of pastoral care was still in its early stages. According to the intensions of Aid to the Church in Need, religious life in God's strongholds should be lived at its highest pitch, so that in these regions of spiritual crisis the presence of the Church might be as intense and impressive as possible. The monastery would be a spiritual centre for the itinerant priests and the Catholics of the whole area. It would offer facilities for retreats and courses; it would also be a social and charitable centre, with shelter for the homeless, *Caritas* depots, kindergartens, sewing schools, hospitals, youth movements and the rest. Besides all this, it was to serve as a base for a group of fervent young chaplains, who would continually crisscross the whole region in their chapel-trucks, always ready to say Mass, preach missions, hear confessions, and give religious instruction. And finally the religious houses were to be considered the advance guard of the Kingdom of God, emphasising and nourishing the Eastern advance of the Church, not in a political or military sense, but in an apostolic one.

This was the vision that unfolded during the first years of Aid to the Church in Need, a vision for which much has been suffered and sacrificed, but which, alas, has been only partially realised.

THE BUILDING COMPANIONS

The "Building Companions" did not grow out of long talks and much theorising, but out of need and love. Need cried out for help, and love found a way. The result was a working community of all those willing to give their time, their strength, their prayers and their money to relieve the housing shortage. Each member pledged himself to pray, to build and to pay.

The idea of a building fraternity came from a meeting I had with a little refugee girl in a refugee camp. I gave the child a holy picture and said she must hang this up on the wall at home. "We haven't got a wall, Father!" she answered. They had no wall! They lived somewhere in the middle of a barracks without walls, without protection against the rawness of life, day and night! It was then that I understood that it would be useless to build convents and churches if the faithful had to be crowded together in squalid mass dwellings, over which the inscription might well be written: "Here the Ten Commandments can no longer be kept!" Without decent dwellings, Christian family life would be lost. And without Christian families, within two generations there would be no Catholicism in these parts: then we would need neither churches nor priests. It was our duty to try to save Christian families: and for that we had to build houses. We had to relieve the housing shortage.

Two men were especially deserving of praise in the realisation of this idea: first, Colonel Van Coppenolle, who carried out the preparatory research in secret and studied the possibility of doing useful work in the housing field with unskilled volunteers. He went to Germany for this purpose in 1952. His well-thought-out reports and expert advice were decisive in the establishment of the Building Companions; the preparation of the first building camp near Münster was chiefly his work.

The second founder of the Building Companions was Fritz Kroeger, the Secretary of the "Christian Masons", who was given several years' leave by the union to sort out the practical organisation of the Building Companions. With his typically German thoroughness, his caution in financial matters and his deep-seated aversion to launching out on risky ventures, he formed an indispensable counterweight in those years to the young Flemings who were the impulsive and dynamic power of the new foundation. To his great credit, he insisted that the building camps should be thoroughly prepared and that the Companions should be properly insured against accidents. He was responsible for the good relations the Companions enjoy with the German bishops, government circles, housing projects and youth organisations. The famous Boniface Housing Estate at Waldkappel, the greatest achievement of the Building Companions, would never have come into existence without the energy, perseverance, wisdom and personal intervention of this, their first leader. He hated superficiality and spectacular experiments. He wanted no cheap popularity. He neglected his own career in order to place the Building Companions on a firm foundation for the next man we entrusted it to: Maurits Nachtergaele, the most energetic and likable publicity agent that ever drove a chapel-truck.

But matters were not so far advanced in 1953, when the Building Companions were just beginning. Nobody believed the idea would work. There was a great deal of opposition, and (despite the encouragement shown by Abbot Stalmans) fierce criticism of the whole adventure. It was only with the assistance of the Jesuit colleges in Flanders that we were able to attempt even a first experiment when, through the good offices of the Jesuit General, a hundred students were placed at our disposal during the Easter vacation of the same year.

The first experiment was called "Münster". There were many displaced persons in the area, living in squalid encampments. They were building their own houses. But it was only by working thousands of hours overtime, with their wives and children, that these destitute people were able to make up for their lack of capital and claim subsidies from the State and credits from the housing fund. A great disadvantage of this self-reliance was the time it took. By the time they left the camp, it was often too late—their families were ruined. Moreover, the poorest of all—the widow with little children, the crippled serviceman with one leg—could not use this method: they simply could not work for thousands of hours.

The task of the first hundred builders, therefore, was to supply ten thousand man-hours in a fortnight, so that the digging of cellars and other preparatory work could advance more rapidly. These hours would chiefly benefit widows and disabled men.

It was a risky undertaking. The farmers of Münsterland were well acquainted with their heavy clay soil and expressed their doubts in no uncertain terms. But the young Flemings started on the work with all the fervour of which they were capable. After three hours of unaccustomed work, the students' hands were covered with bruises and blisters—but nobody gave in. That night, as the boys slept exhausted on their straw pallets, the farmers inspected the building site with stable lanterns to see what these boys from Flanders had managed. They could not say that they had done a bad job, and they would not admit that it was a fine achievement. So they said nothing at all. But they thought, "Tomorrow there will be less."

The second evening, the farmers found with astonishment that the young builders had done twice as much work as the day before. On the third day there were not enough wheelbarrows and carts to carry away the earth. Then, in the afternoon, the first farmer appeared with a horse and cart to help. The next day, there were seven farmers on the building site with horses and carts, sons and farmhands.

The example of those hundred hard-working boys stirred the whole district to action. Soon farmers and refugees, students and town-dwellers were working side by side with the white-clad builders in the heavy soil of Münsterland. By the end of a fortnight, so much had been done that forty-eight families were able to move into their houses a year sooner than had been expected. Among them were thirteen families who, without the assistance of the young builders, would never have been able to sleep under a roof of their own.

The experiment was a success.

The work was extended at once. In that same year, 1953, many other experiments were made with groups of unemployed, with undergraduates, schoolboys, and workers from Belgium and the Netherlands. All the building camps were completely financed beforehand by the Building Companions organisation set up in Germany with capital furnished by Aid to the Church in Need, with the exception of a contribution to the travelling expenses paid by the participants themselves. We helped the settlers and the itinerant priests free of charge.

The Belgian building camps or *chantiers* helped to build a large number of German churches. About five hundred people had joined their ranks, and their enthusiasm—and the results—exceeded all hopes. The Flemish campaign owned twenty building camps with more than six hundred members, and concentrated on building houses for the very poorest. As early as September 1953, eleven hundred Dutch and Belgian volunteer builders in the refugee areas proved the viability of the Building Companions.

The Building Companions were founded for the purpose of pastoral care. When ACN sent its chapel-trucks and Vehicles for God swarming out to the refugee areas, there began a period of closer contact with the Catholics scattered throughout the vast Protestant country. Hundreds of priests were given the opportunity to discover the deep distress among the displaced Germans. Within a short time the alarm bells were ringing in Tongerlo.

Itinerant priests and chapel-truck missionaries agreed unanimously that the young Catholic communities would be able to keep alive in this bleak spiritual climate only if each family had a secure home and God had a dwelling in the midst of His people. The Christian

PLATE 20. Blessing the rafters in Waldkappel. The Building Order founded by Father Werenfried built countless churches for God and houses for the homeless in the emergency zones in God's Kingdom.

community grows round the altar, and the Christian family cannot flourish in the midst of crowds.

This was our motive for summoning the volunteer builders to construct houses for the people and churches for God, wherever the Kingdom of God was threatened by a shortage of houses and churches. In our first publication about this new enterprise of ACN, we stressed its ecclesiastical character and expressed our fervent hope that out of the community of Building Companions would spring a secular institute of permanent Building Brothers to serve this social and pastoral need in the Church. This group of Building Brothers consecrated to God would become the head and heart of the organisation. To preserve the apostolic character of the Building Companions and to preserve unity between temporary and permanent members, it would, of course, be essential that the whole Institute remained under ecclesiastical leadership.

It had always been our intention that the temporary Building Companions should be attached to the Building Brothers as a kind of Third Order, a socio-religious movement within this Institute, so that they would be able to pursue their common purpose under the spiritual and technical guidance of the permanent members.

The temporary Companions who place themselves at the disposal of the Church in distress for a few weeks in the year serve to a lesser degree the same ideal as that to which the Building Brothers, bound by vows, devote their whole lives. The temporary workers are, however, indispensable because they donate their time and efforts, which makes it possible to realise great objectives at little expense. They also form the natural soil from which the

Secular Institute can obtain vocations. Finally, they lay the economic foundations of the Secular Institute by their monetary contributions.

I once had a vision of the International Building Institute as an institution of the Church in the service of God's Kingdom. This dream has not been realised. As with every new foundation, patience and time are needed—and there are always human imperfections and errors to be reckoned with. There were difficulties and misunderstandings. But greater than these were the honest intentions and goodwill of many thousands of volunteer builders and of about twenty Building Brothers—and the Grace of God. And so I thank God for the Building Companions; for their marvellous beginnings and their great achievements; for the generosity and sacrifice, the love and the sorrow, that were poured into this foundation.

Undoubtedly the Building Companions have accomplished marvels in the material field. Many thousands have experienced the great benefit of the help given by these volunteer builders. The moral and psychological value of this glorious campaign was, however, much greater. The presence of volunteer builders in hundreds of towns and villages cast bridges across the frontiers. Their example provoked admiration, and imitation. Valuable contacts were made, prejudices were removed, friendships were formed. The builders learned to serve in a community; they learned respect for manual labour; their outlook was broadened. A number of them found their vocation to the priesthood in response to the spiritual necessity that confronted them. Many priests declared that the self-denial, the example and the Christian testimony of these boys did more good among their flock than a popular mission would have done.

The Building Brothers! Over the years one group has replaced another, but all working at the same enthusiastic rhythm. They wielded their pickaxes and shovels, they bent their backs to the digging, they sweated under the weight of heavy stones. They sawed wood, laid bricks and poured concrete. They sang their songs, each in his own language; they laughed and fraternised with each other; they made eyes at the girls; and they prayed seriously and thoughtfully before their work and during the daily community Mass, so that God might bless their efforts. The story of this work was told in a book called *Hands of God*: a rugged story, but a beautiful one. Foul weather often called for heroism, and there was heroism: only God knows how much good that did.

The spirit of the Building Companions is the spirit of action, service, inventive love, diligence for souls and modern apostleship. This was the spirit we tried to sketch out in the "rule" that we drew up for the Building Companions in 1953:

> Admitted as "companions" are young men from 17 to 30 who are healthy in body and mind and are willing to volunteer their labour to build dwellings for displaced persons and the homeless and build churches and monasteries in any district to which ecclesiastical authorities may summon them. They bind themselves to the following conditions.
>
> 1. The Building Companion works for eight hours a day without wages on the building site to which he is assigned by the authorities of the Building Institute. He is to follow the instructions of the foreman. He must

be aware that he is at the service of the poor and the destitute, in whom Christ is personified, as He Himself said: "Inasmuch as you have done it to the least of My brethren you have done it unto Me." Therefore he will fulfil with love, diligence and care the task allotted to him, which must, however, be suited to his ability and bodily strength.

2. The Building Companion is part of a group and is thus jointly responsible for the healthy atmosphere in this group. He will therefore be diligent, self-sacrificing, honest, sobre and tolerant, helping his companions by his example. He will not seek his own profit, but will serve the others.

3. The Companion will place himself under the spiritual guidance of the chaplain, whose job it is to keep the team spirit at a high level and free from bad influences. The Companion will find in the chaplain a counsellor and friend.

4. The Companion follows his group leader in everything he asks for the welfare of the group, remembering always that there can be no order if everyone follows his own judgment. The Companion must, therefore, be able to renounce his own plans and ideas.

The group leader must be an example for all. He is to be the servant of all, especially of those who are less able. He will discuss with the chaplain the interests of the group and make the necessary decisions.

5. The Companion is aware that in the midst of needy people he is the representative of Holy Church, to which he bears witness by his Christian way of life. His example may be a signpost to God for erring souls.

Besides the work of his hands, he will give to these people also his interest in their needs and problems. He must be able to listen patiently to the story of their suffering. In order to approach these people, he should not let false shame prevent him from speaking their language, however brokenly.

6. The Companion can be sure that the Building Institute will settle all technical details for him. The Institute will insure him against accidents during his travel and at work. It will provide transportation and passports, accommodation and working clothes and also first aid.

7. The Companion will be pleasant and cheerful during recreation hours, gladly offering his gifts and accomplishments for the amusement of others. He will remember that even in song and recreation the honour and dignity of his people must be maintained abroad; he will sing only decent songs, speak in a civilised way and not demean himself by lewdness and coarseness. In everything he will radiate the nobility and high spirits of the children of God.

8. The Companion fulfils his task in an apostolic spirit. He will work for the security and extension of the Kingdom of God upon earth, helped by the pastoral care of Holy Church. Therefore he will seek strength and inspiration in Christ, who gave His life for souls. His prayers will be disciplined, manly and without false modesty. He will find his strength in the Holy Mass and the sacraments, through which Christ will fill him with His living strength.

This was the project of the Building Companions planned in cooperation with Abbot Emilius Stalmans, who died during the first building camp at Münster. This was no new volunteer labour service, which, together with a hundred other organisations of a like nature, would be benevolently tolerated in UNESCO circles, but a fighting legion of young lay apostles under the leadership and in the service of the Church, inspired by a consecrated nucleus of technically skilled Building Brothers, who were prepared to realise the material conditions for the growth of God's Kingdom by building all over the world. Their marching orders were to the underdeveloped countries, missions and, after the collapse of the Communist dictatorships, the countries behind the Iron Curtain.

It was decided by my Superior in September 1960 that I should no longer have to accept any moral or financial responsibility for the Building Companions. In my position as their founder, however, I have once more emphasised in these pages the ideal that I had in mind at the time, and which, as a parting gift, I entrust to the hands and hearts of my brave Building Companions.

FROM THE 2ND TO
THE 9TH OF JANUARY

From a human point of view, Aid to the Church in Need's world-wide activity is an enigma. Heaven knows that the sickly monk who was entrusted with this work possessed neither the physical strength nor the wisdom nor the many other virtues and talents that common sense tells us are indispensable for such a task. More than anyone else I am convinced that in this case God chose a weak, foolish and unworthy tool to bring about a great enterprise. Without the frequent and specific intervention of God, it would long ago have perished under the weight of the wickedness or stupidity of others, and of myself—so that it is to Him and Him only that all the honour and glory belong.

After having experienced God's blessing, helping us or saving us in the most difficult situations over so many years, we cannot in the long run distinguish where trust in God ends and recklessness begins. Perhaps it is not even important to know this, as it is apparently very difficult for God to betray an unshakeable trust in Him, even when, by human standards, it must be called foolhardy. When we read the parable of the man who woke his friend up in the middle of the night in order to borrow a loaf of bread, we are inclined to call his action outrageous, while to God it is apparently nothing more than a persevering and confident prayer. Christ did not even hesitate to hold up this night-time disturber as an example to us. While many Christians would call this kind of faith extravagant, God's view is undoubtedly the proper one; therefore it seems that we should not be overly influenced in our faith by the kind of wisdom that is probably "of this world". Instead of letting difficulties hold us up, we honour God much more by leaving the solution of these difficulties to Him and fearlessly starting to act.

To illustrate this trust in God, I shall relate how I was forced to found the Secular Institute of the Building Brothers between the 2nd and the 9th of January. Soon after the first building camps, I received letters and visits from young men who wished to devote their whole lives to the ideal of the temporary builders. They were prepared to take vows in a spiritual institution to be founded by me. I hesitated for a long time: it was a heavy responsibility to induce young people to renounce everything and choose a way of life that did not yet exist and that they would have to shape for themselves. Ought I begin such a thing without the inner certainty that it was God's will? I must honestly admit that I found it difficult to see myself in the light of a founder of a religious order. When I compared myself secretly with the serious men who had undertaken such work in earlier times, I was filled with terror. I decided, then, not to hurry matters, and asked the candidates to be patient. They waited patiently for a year and a half, and then entered the Jesuit Order or a mission congregation as a lay brother. These are, no doubt, fine vocations, but I would have preferred to have had them in the Building Institute. Nevertheless, I did not dare to take the decisive step until, on 2nd January 1956, I received a letter from the convent of the Poor Clares in Düsseldorf.

Some time before I had given the nuns in that convent a talk on Aid to the Church in Need. Motionless and attentive, they had listened to my story of the spiritual and material distress out in the great, strange world where everything was so different from their well-protected life behind grilles and convent walls. After the meeting I was invited, like every preacher of retreats and recollections, to the parlour for a sandwich, a cup of tea and a talk with the Reverend Mother. She asked me to explain about our Fortresses for God in Germany and wanted to know whether Aid to the Church in Need also built convents for contemplatives.

I said that we had not done so hitherto, but that it was an attractive idea. We had built religious houses for active priests full of apostolic zeal, who raced throughout their areas by car, preaching, celebrating Mass and hearing confessions from early morning to late at night; and who—naturally enough—had little time for formal times of prayer, meditation, or extraordinary penances. This feverish way of life seemed justified, on account of the bitter spiritual need of the people for whom they had been ordained priests, but on the other hand it required a counterbalance of a more spiritual and contemplative nature. So even though it was impossible, in our troubled times, to obtain the right mixture of contemplation and action in the life of every priest, yet there ought to be at least a division of labour in the great organism of the Mystical Body and in every great province of the Kingdom of God, so as to do justice to each of these two indispensable aspects of the Christian life. There must, then, be no lack of contemplative communities to back up the select troops of the active pastors. Without doubt, the presence of religious spending their lives in prayer and atonement would be a source of blessing and grace both for the refugees and for their itinerant pastors. For these reasons I assured the Reverend Mother that I was prepared, as a matter of principle, to get together the money for a contemplative bastion of prayer, if she in her turn would supply the nuns necessary to populate the convent. She undertook to do this without hesitation, and until the beginning of 1955 we had repeated conversations about our proposal to found a convent of Poor Clares in the German diaspora.

Now I must admit that I have a bad memory. In those days I quite frequently preached up to a hundred sermons a month in places scattered over half of Europe; I was continuously on the road, and I escaped far too frequently from the watchful care of the excellent secretary who was, for years, my conscience and my memory, and who would remind me at regular intervals of the promises I had made (as I was in the habit of doing, in the spirit of trust in God that I have indicated above). Added to this was the difficulty that she could not possibly know what appointments I had made during my journeys, so that with the best will in the world, she could not prevent some things from getting into a hopeless muddle. One of those things was the project I had discussed in Düsseldorf and which, to my great shame, I completely forgot about afterwards.

Suddenly, on 2nd January 1956—to the surprise of all concerned—a letter from the Reverend Mother landed on my desk. She wanted to know what further steps were being taken in the matter of our contemplative foundation. Triumphantly she informed me that a rich sinner (who is without sin?) was willing to make a gift of a suitable piece of ground, and that a pious architect was willing to draw up the plans for nothing. Besides this, the little convent in Düsseldorf was overcrowded— there were plenty of new vocations—so there was no time to lose. Discreetly she suggested that my silence might be the result of Aid to the Church in Need's lack of funds, in which case she asked whether the Building Companions might not perhaps be put to work.

In my reply, sent off on the same day, I promised her that Aid to the Church in Need would keep its word, although at that moment we had indeed neither money nor a proper Building Institute. I explained to her that a convent could not be built with volunteer temporary builders, but that I had for a long time had the idea of founding a kind of "Secular Institute of Building Brothers" that would put the finishing touch to the Building Companions. These permanent Brothers—bricklayers, carpenters, electricians, engineers and architects—would naturally be in a position to build the convent we had promised. However, before I could call up the waiting candidates, four conditions would have to be fulfilled. In the first place, there would have to be a bishop to bless the new Institute and to give his approval for its foundation. In the second place, winter quarters were needed where the Brothers could receive their spiritual training and technical education during the idle season. In the third place, we could not begin without a pious and experienced priest to whom I could entrust the spiritual guidance of the Institute; and in the fourth place, at least one of the prospective Brothers must have the qualities needed to become eventually the Superior of the Institute. I added: "If you and your Sisters can pray so well that these four conditions are fulfilled *within the week*, this will be for me a sign from Heaven that I must found the Secular Institute of Building Brothers. I promise you that in that case the Novices of the Institute will build your convent and that Aid to the Church in Need will find the funds for the building material."

This is what I wrote on 2nd January 1956, the first day of a week full of miracles. On 4th January, I received a call from Pietro Modesto, an Italian who at that time represented our work in Vienna. He informed me that Aid to the Church in Need had been offered an estate in Carinthia, in the Karawank Mountains (on the Yugoslav border), consisting of two mountain tops with a small church, a farm, a house, and a forest. He thought we might perhaps turn it into a holiday resort for aged refugees from the Austrian camps. They could live in the house, live on the farm produce, bring with them a priest in need of rest to say Mass in the old chapel, and we could chop down a few trees every year to pay for travelling expenses. The house would, however, need some repairs to be made suitable for its new purpose. Could I send over a group of Building Companions as soon as possible?

The thought suddenly shot through my mind that this offer would solve the problem of winter quarters for the Building Brothers. If they spent the first winter of their novitiate there, the mountain tops could still serve as a holiday resort in the summer. The house would therefore be productive the whole year round. Moreover, the Building Brothers would then have something to do. It is impossible to keep young men active for the whole winter with just spiritual exercises, meditations, lessons on the spiritual life, foreign languages and the theory of craftsmanship: for many of them this would be the shortest road to the lunatic asylum. But in the winter quarters of Sankt Florian (this was the name of the hamlet), they could alternate their spiritual programme with physical labour. They would be able to restore the house and chapel, help at the farm and fell trees in the woods. And as soon as the building season began, they would make room for the refugees escaping from the desolate atmosphere of life in the camps to recuperate for a few months at the expense of our Organisation.

Without delay I authorised Pietro Modesto to arrange everything in Sankt Florian and to get into touch with the Bishop of Klagenfurt to obtain his blessing and approval for the setting-up of the novitiate. On 6th January, I was informed by telegram that the bishop was willing. Thus we had both our bishop and our winter quarters. On 7th January, I phoned Franz, one of the best of the candidates and a man without whom I was not willing to start on this adventurous enterprise. I asked him if he was prepared to become a Building Brother in February. Franz had been waiting for two years for our Institute to be set up; but he had his own responsibilities as the leader of a Boys' Home, and could hardly just set aside his duties at the drop of a hat. First he would have to find someone to look after his boys. He pleaded for a few months' delay. I urged him to come immediately, and told him quite plainly that the foundation could not take place without him. Franz repeated that he could not promise anything at such short notice, and told me that he would explain his reason fully in writing. This was a real disappointment.

Nevertheless I went to my Abbot on 8th January (not Abbot Stalmans, who had died in 1953, but his successor), and asked him to appoint one of my colleagues as spiritual director of the new foundation. The Abbot looked slightly perplexed when I explained to him my plans with regard to the Secular Institute of the Building Brothers. Understandably, it was difficult for him to imagine that a bacon-begging priest should also be called upon to become the founder of a religious order. But he listened quite patiently as I told him how these plans had come about, and what had happened since 2nd January. He smiled faintly when I told him that Franz, the indispensable leader-in-potential, would probably not be able to join.

He told me: "You've made your Foundation dependent on four conditions, and you may start only if all of them are fulfilled. If Franz joins, I'll give you a spiritual director from the Abbey and you can send the first group of Building Brothers to Sankt Florian in February. But if he doesn't join, you won't get your novice master and you'll have to put the whole Institute idea out of your head, because the four conditions won't have been fulfilled and you won't have got the 'sign from heaven' you were waiting for". It was a pretty definite decision, and, in view of my telephone conversation with Franz, it seemed a fairly definite negative.

The next morning, 9th January, the letter from Franz arrived, and it was one of the most miraculous events that I have ever experienced. It read as follows:

Almost immediately after our phone conversation, I received the visit of an old friend whom I had not seen for six years. He used to be the leader of a boys' home like me, and he came to ask me if I could recommend him a position, as he was out of work at the moment. I gave him my own job, so I am now free to become a Building Brother in February. I am bringing another candidate.

Success! I went straight to the abbot with this letter. He was even more astonished than the day before. He shook his head, but he kept his promise and gave me the spiritual director that I needed. Thus in just one week we had obtained winter quarters, a bishop, Franz and a spiritual director. Through the insistent prayers of a little-known convent of Poor Clares, the four conditions stipulated on 2nd January were fulfilled before 9th January, and I was given the go-ahead for the adventure of Sankt Florian.

In February, the first Building Brothers left for Austria under the leadership of my own former novice master. High up on the mountains, in snow and cold, they prayed, worked and fought for their vocations. They were given their religious instruction, and with the aid of an old record player they struggled to learn German. They restored the little church and made the house habitable for vacationers. They helped on the farm and felled a hundred and fifty trees, by accident, in the wrong forest! But God is not miserly with His blessings, and the owner let us keep the trees. The sum for which they were sold covered all the expenses of the first winter quarters.

The simple convent of the Poor Clares built by the Building Brothers as a bastion of prayer and as a memorial to that miraculous week has now been standing for some time in the neighbourhood of Hanover. It is a memorial to the week from 2nd to 9th January to which the Secular Institute of the Building Brothers owes its existence.

HUNGARIAN TRAGEDY

Friday, 26th October 1956; ten o'clock at night. The radio news bulletin brings the first news of the Hungarian revolt: "Two hundred and fifty wounded people have arrived at Nickelsdorf on the Austro-Hungarian frontier."

In the headquarters of ACN at Tongerlo, the news is passed on to me immediately. Ten minutes later I am on my way to Louvain with Staf Vermeulen, the director of our Organisation in Belgium. In Louvain we hold a council of war at half past eleven with the Jesuit Father Laszlo Varga, advisor for our Hungarian section. The very same night our marvellous Hungary campaign begins.

Saturday, 27th October; five o'clock in the afternoon. The first Sabena plane is on its way with a thousand bottles of blood plasma from the Red Cross and a precious consignment of medical supplies from Aid to the Church in Need. All friends and helpers have already been warned. The first appeals have appeared in the evening papers.

But first of all came prayer. In the night between Saturday and Sunday, at midnight, sixty of us gathered in the Place Rogier in Brussels to pray the Rosary. A fine rain was falling. We walked past sleeping houses and dripping trees. The wind rattled the iron gates and played with the wet leaves. Praying aloud, we marched through Avenue Churchill to the Hungarian legation, a large mansion with a small garden in front. All the shutters were closed. We knelt on the cobblestones and prayed together for the persecuted Church, for the fighters on the barricades of Budapest, for the mothers, wives and children in terror for the lives of their husbands, fathers and sons. We prayed for friends and for enemies.

Then came the police, fearing demonstrations and bombs. They were surprised at this praying of the Rosary on the wet ground in nocturnal Brussels and wanted to prohibit it. Reinforcements came along, a jeep full of heavily armed gendarmes. We went on praying, Rosary after Rosary, in the dim light of the street lamps.

When we had finished with the Hungarian legation we went to the Bulgarian one, then to the Polish consulate in Avenue Molière and on to the Russian embassy. We knelt and prayed as if there were no houses, no people, no policemen. There were only a few of us, a small, spontaneous, private enterprise, but it would grow. In the weeks to come it would grow into a storm of prayers blowing through all the parishes of Flanders. Hundreds of thousands would take part in it. It would become grand and impressive, but never again would it be so moving as on that first night when, at the head of a small group of fellow workers, I walked through the rain in sleeping Brussels to unleash the revolution of prayer.

In the warehouse in Tongerlo the machinery had been set in motion. The offices were transformed into a dispensary. In that first Saturday night, about eleven o'clock, young pharmacists, summoned by telegramme, began to sort mountains of bottles, ampoules and boxes.

PLATE 21. Brussels, October 1956. A prayer vigil in front of the Eastern European embassies during the Hungarian uprising.

In the warehouse the packed parcels were piling up: vitamins, bandages, antibiotics, quinine, pain-killers. The same thing was happening in Antwerp and throughout Flanders, where our fellow workers were busy in schools, halls and warehouses. By Sunday morning the Hungarian campaign was snowballing into an avalanche. Many hospitals had sent a good part of their medical supplies to our warehouses. Throughout the whole country, volunteer helpers requisitioned cars to drive from house to house. The Hungarian frontier was open: Aid to the Church in Need entered the breach and pressed into the lands behind the Iron Curtain, with hands full of charity.

Monday. No way of estimating the extent of the campaign. Yet chaos was overcome with neighbourly love, faith—and improvisation. During the night a plane chartered by *Caritas* and Aid to the Church in Need taxied onto the runway at Melsbroek. The engines revved up, and two and a half tons of medical supplies soared into the air. With this cargo, six large hospitals can carry on for a week. At the same time, the lights were still burning in the storerooms of ACN at Tongerlo, as twenty-five tons of clothes, shoes and foodstuffs were loaded onto our twenty-ton truck. At four o'clock the next morning, Heinz drove the full truck out of the warehouse. An hour later a driver in the neighbourhood of St. Gall put his foot on the accelerator of his Mercedes: twelve tons of gift parcels from ACN in Switzerland, bound for Vienna. Everywhere our own or borrowed transport was mobilised. From ten cities throughout Western Europe, the tangible help and charity of our benefactors were on the way to Hungary.

On Tuesday morning I took the plane to Vienna. The news of the uprising was increasingly favourable, and Cardinal Mindszenty was expected to be released soon. In Vienna we consulted with our local workers and other organisations. They were cautious and wanted to wait: I decided to start immediately. I had no valid passport or visa, only my Rosary. I prayed the Rosary with my Austrian and Hungarian friends from Vienna to Budapest. The adventure was a success: three hours after his liberation I stood with the chairman of the Austrian *Caritas* and a few others, in a small room, with Cardinal Mindszenty. We were the first priests from the West to see him. The revolution was still going on.

Indeed, the revolution was at its height. At Nickelsdorf, on the Austrian border, workers were standing armed with rifles. Everywhere we met cars draped with the Hungarian flag—with the Soviet red star cut out. In Györ, there were tanks in front of the house of the bishop we visited. He had often heard of Aid to the Church in Need and took the opportunity to ask me for a truckload of gift parcels for his diocese: we were happy to oblige. Thanks to this promise, our last truck did not drive on to Budapest, but stopped in Györ to be unloaded. If it had not done so, both truck and driver would have fallen into the hands of the Russians. As it was, Heinz, the last in the convoy, was only just able to escape from Hungary: five minutes after our cavalcade had passed Nickelsdorf, the frontier was sealed by Soviet armoured troops.

But on All Saints' Day, when we drove to Budapest full of hope, things had not come to such a pass. There was fighting going on here and there. The people along

PLATE 22. Cardinal Mindszenty, Primate of Hungary, after his release at the time of the Hungarian uprising (1 November 1956).

the roads waved to us, and everywhere flags were flying from the houses. It was a national revolt; the whole population was full of enthusiasm. We arrived in Budapest towards evening. In the suburbs we saw more and more black flags on the houses: these had their dead to mourn. The city was a terrible sight. There were burnt-out Russian tanks everywhere. Here and there a tram-car formed a barricade across a street. There were ruined houses and incredible quantities of torn-up documents on the square in front of the public buildings. The suburbs were patrolled by trucks full of freedom fighters: young fellows with thin, weary faces under helmets too large for them. There was still shooting going on in the distance. Children were riding on the tanks of the rebellious Hungarian army. Two tightly closed Soviet tanks left the city under the threatening eyes of the population.

We found the badly-damaged dwelling of the Cardinal without much difficulty. All the corridors and rooms were full of people lining up to welcome the liberated Prince of the Church; we pushed our way through the crowd and entered a front room. There were a couple of bishops, some officers and many poorly dressed civilians waiting to see the Cardinal.

Most had come straight from prison. For years they had suffered persecution for the Faith; now they came to offer their services for the reconstruction of Church life. I noted down dozens of addresses, with the idea of sending them a gift packet from Aid to the Church in Need later on. But nothing came of that idea. Some of them I saw a few weeks later as refugees: most of them were executed by the triumphant Communists. May they rest in peace!

The Cardinal received us with great emotion. He was stooping, unshaven and poorly dressed. He had black hair, a slow, heavy voice, an energetic manner and penetrating eyes that moved quickly from one visitor to another. He spoke in German.

I told him about the campaign that we had been preparing for the day of liberation, about our chapel-trucks, about spiritual and material relief that we would be able to bring, about the plans we had drawn up with Bishop Adam, Bishop Zagon, Bishop Mester, Father Varga and other spiritual leaders of the Hungarian emigrés for the future of the Church in this martyred country. He listened attentively, asked for an explanation here and there and enlightened his secretary on some points in Hungarian. He sent for a certain monsignor and appointed him there and then to be president of Catholic Action, with the assignment of accepting the charitable help of the Western European Church and distributing it throughout Hungary. He was surprised at the generous offer of help that Monsignor Pfeiffer, the undaunted president of Austrian *Caritas*, also made.

Then he retired to write a letter to his fellow bishops for us to take with us. The letter read as follows:

To the Catholic bishops of the world!

I was moved to learn how much the Catholics of the whole world sympathise with the sorely afflicted Hungarian people.

Our necessity and poverty being very great, I ask my fellow bishops of the Catholic Church to appeal to their faithful to put their neighbourly love into practice and send help to the Hungarian Catholic *Caritas*.

The Hungarian people, so few in number, are now carrying on the historical mission entrusted to us five hundred years ago at the victory of Belgrade.

For the generous help given up to now, I hereby express my heartfelt thanks.

On the first day of my regained liberty I send the Catholic bishops of the world my greetings in brotherly love from the capital of Hungary.

József Mindszenty
Budapest
31st October 1956

He handed us the letter, and we promised to send it on. When I took leave of him, he clasped my two hands in his and said:

"Father, when you return to the West, tell your friends that they are not to forget us. Ask them to pray, to keep on praying. For there is a difficult struggle ahead of us."

The Cardinal knew what lay ahead. When I left the capital, there were candles burning in all the windows for the twenty thousand dead of Budapest. But in spite of these bloody sacrifices, the people were cheerful and glad because they thought, then, that the end of their way of the cross had come. And then I grew afraid. Not for myself, but for this courageous people that with its simple working men, with its children and students, had fought so bravely and so entirely alone against overwhelming force. These people, who were still under the delusion that things would now improve, did not yet know that the Cardinal had grasped my two hands and begged me to pray, to keep on praying for the difficult struggle that was still ahead of them.

On All Saints' Day we left the country, unharmed. We translated the Cardinal's letter, sent it to the bishops, and published it in the press. We begged a sum of almost two million dollars for the Mindszenty Fund. We distributed enormous quantities of gift parcels in Hungary and to the Hungarian refugees everywhere in Europe. We had hundreds of thousands of Hungarian catechisms, prayer books and Bibles printed, and were even able to send a great amount of them into Hungary during the weeks of confusion during and after the revolt. Aid to the Church in Need—the only organisation that specialises in relief for the persecuted Church—stood, at the time of the Hungarian tragedy and during the months that followed, at the forefront of all the campaigns that were started with such generosity all over the world.

But the best contribution that our countless friends then made was the "storm" novena of the Rosary, which for months kept consciences awake and, in spite of the apparent failure of the revolt, brought about without any doubt miracles of grace and blessings in Hungary.

What had been begun in the cobbled streets of Brussels that night spread like wildfire. The next to follow was Bruges, with a Rosary procession to the chapel of the Precious Blood. In one week the cathedral of Antwerp was four times filled to overflowing with praying men and women, boys and girls, who added a sacrifice to their prayers. In Lokeren the mayor and aldermen led the procession, and on that Rosary evening their city collected seventy-five thousand francs for Hungary for the Mindszenty Fund. In Louvain fifteen thousand students and citizens marched praying through the streets to Bishop Van Vayenberg's open-air evening Mass, and they collected three hundred thousand francs for the Hungarian Church in distress. Antwerp, Kiel, Mortsel, Bouchout, St. Nicholas, Dendermonde—from all these places rose a whirlwind of Rosaries and self-sacrifice. In the Antwerp parish of the Holy Ghost, one Sunday morning, three hundred sixty-seven thousand francs were collected for the relief fund of Aid to the Church in Need. And all this was only a small part of the campaign carried on during that first week after my return from Budapest.

During those days even Belgian Radio, exceptionally, placed its microphone at the disposal of Aid to the Church in Need. I took advantage of it to rouse the people for our prayer campaign.

> The world is on fire. The Church is bleeding. Christ is dying in people without number. Do we know what is at stake? Will our churches be full of imploring Christians tomorrow and the day after? Have we meditated on the reasons why God allows this terrible affliction? Do all, even the very least of us, try to persuade Our Lord? Do we *keep on* storming Him with prayers, crying out loudly to Heaven? Will we persevere in our attempts to propitiate Him with prayers and sacrifices?

> Humanly speaking it is hopeless. Do not think that the Western powers will lift a finger to save liberty in Hungary. Do not believe for a moment that the gentlemen who attacked Suez are truly interested in the Church in distress! Wake up! Admit that all human means are inadequate, and that God alone is able to save.

> God alone can save. This is a cold shower for our pride; it is humiliating for modern humanity. Yet it

is no cause for fear, for God is the only "Ally" who is truly disinterested. His way of rescuing is different from any human solution, but it is safer, more lasting and infinitely better.

God alone can save. This is the conclusion that has always followed from mistakes and lost illusions, the realisation that was gained after all other methods had failed. The Jews of the Old Covenant knew it, but they knew it only in the Babylonian captivity. And the menaced Christianity of centuries ago only discovered it when the Turks had reached the heart of Europe.

We, too, must learn it at the eleventh hour, and it will give us peace of mind. We should not think it a risk to trust in the Lord, in the almighty, strong God, Who laughs the heathens to scorn and breaks them to pieces like a potter's vessel. It is not alarming to build on Him alone, for He has conquered the world. Let us therefore beseech Him with our childlike faith and with the surge of our prayers beating on His listening Heart. . . .

Day after day, and many times a day, I spoke about the Hungarian mothers fleeing with their children, just as Mary had fled before Herod.

The refugee mother arriving in the frontier camp of Traiskirchen in Austria and photographed feeding her child is burdened with the same care and the same sorrow as Mary once bore.

That other mother—her picture was in the papers—with the weary face, exhausted after carrying her child for many miles on her back, between bundles of clothes, is as tired as Mary was when she rested during the flight into Egypt.

And another refugee mother, also shown in the newspaper—who knows her name?—with eyes full of terror, is as afraid as Mary was when she heard the wailing of the mothers in Bethlehem behind her.

And the many Hungarian mothers who lost their children when the whole village scattered at the approach of the raging tanks are now being tortured this very day—tortured by a thousand terrors just as Mary was when on leaving Jerusalem she found she had lost Jesus.

And the weeping mothers, older than those others, who watched while their grown sons were herded together and carried away to an unknown destination. In the hearts of these mothers is the same sorrow as the heart of Mary felt when her divine Son was led away by the soldiers out of the Garden of Olives.

And the mothers of Budapest who see their sons hanging from the street lamps are like the Mother of Sorrows, whose heart was transfixed by a sword under her Son's cross.

And those mothers who search through the ruins and among the wreckage of the burnt-out tanks, if they find their dead child after a while, will be like Mary, weeping, with Jesus in her lap, murdered, pale and cold. You thousands of poor, hunted, ravaged and outcast mothers of Hungary, we cannot do much for you. We have only our inadequate love and our prayers. But we can entrust you to Mary, who knows all your pains, having experienced them herself, who understands you as no one else can and who alone can comfort you in these bitterest hours of your lives.

The Hungarian revolt, with its aftermath of tens of thousands of refugees, opened the eyes and hearts of innumerable people to the distress of the persecuted Church. Western Christendom learned again to pray for the sixty million oppressed brothers in Hungary and other satellite states, deformed by an evil government and estranged from us by the Iron Curtain. But we were also faced with unexpected problems.

The years of Communist terror, propaganda and education did not pass without leaving their mark on our brothers in the Faith. The Iron Curtain had increased not only the geographical but also the psychological distance between East and West. For after 1945 the great Christian community, which had already suffered so much from the Schism and the Reformation, was separated once more by the barricades of the Iron Curtain. And even if the Iron Curtain should disappear, the disruption will continue! The Hungarian revolt was certainly a slap in the face to Communism, but it did not prove that there was one living Church community, for East and West have lost touch with each other.

In the "Hungarian People's Democracy", it was the elite of the working-class who revolted in the name of freedom, of the individuality of man and of social justice against the Marxist dictatorship of lies. They were the loyalest of the loyal, the carefully picked and thousand-fold-tested group of young intellectuals. They were the Communist leaders of the workers in the state industries. It was the men in charge and the future leaders of State and Party who rebelled against Moscow. They were the young men who were supposed to have been made fire-proof in the furnaces of dialectic, Marxists who had suddenly seen through Marxism and unmasked it as a fraud to deceive the people.

They were not Titoists, or national Communists, or Socialists or Fascists; but they were not Christians either. They had as yet no name. They were what comes after

PLATE 23. Catholic students in Louvain taking part in a night-time prayer procession during the brutal repression of the Hungarian uprising in 1956.

PLATE 24. More than two thousand students from the Catholic University of Louvain donated blood for the wounded in Hungary. Flemish students bring their gifts to the trucks of Aid to the Church in Need.

Communism—the antithesis born of the thesis of Communism, and therefore necessarily the bitter enemies of a point of view they regarded as out of date.

These *post*-Communists who fought Communism, who saw clearly and hungered and thirsted for righteousness, love and truth—for everything of which Communism is the negation—these young counter-revolutionaries are our brethren who were stolen away from the Church, or who perhaps never belonged to it, yet they belong on our side and we must unceasingly include them in our prayers and in our love.

But let us have no illusions. What follows after Communism cannot simply be annexed by the Church. Those who have passed through the melting pot of Communism cannot simply be incorporated into the old Mother Church as a matter of mere quantitative increase: first *we* must improve our quality. Millions of rebels in Eastern Europe have inwardly conquered Marxism. We can be united with them in truth only if we can overcome our own materialism. As long as we have not reached this stage, we will have no lessons, no good advice to give to these post-Communists, and we would do better to learn ourselves, from them, how to live in self-sacrifice and to die for an ideal.

The revolt failed. The breach in the Iron Curtain closed again. But in our midst there are refugees, young men who can show us in their own persons what those who have passed through the school of Communism are like. Sometimes they are better than we are; but they have been disfigured and deformed. They themselves are not responsible for the damage done to their souls. But at any rate they are a type of human being whom we have to take into account, the type we shall find everywhere in the East after the liberation, and with whom we shall have to form a community. The Hungarian revolt will not have been in vain if *we* draw our lessons from it.

Millions of people in Eastern Europe struggle daily to be inwardly free of the terror and despotism of the Evil One. Millions passionately seek the truth and belong already, by baptism of desire or baptism of blood, to the Church of Christ. Let us pray often for these brethren of ours in the East, that the Lord may soon set them free and lead them to us in peace. But let us also pray for ourselves, that the Lord may purify us, so that our lack of Christian spirit may not stand in the way of reunion with those purified by suffering and seeking the truth.

THE NIGHT YUSSEF DIED

I was in the Holy Land on ACN business, in the country where hills, roads and villages are marked by the footsteps of the Saviour, where Jesus and His mother smiled and where they wept; the wasted vineyard where God was in agony, and where even now the Church undergoes the passion and death of the Crucified in her members; the goal of pilgrims and penitents for more than nineteen hundred years; scene of the holy yet sinful adventures of the Crusades and of young Israel returning to the Promised Land of its fathers loaded with the blessings and curses of modern civilisation.

This country is visited by many Jewish refugees, businessmen and tourists, but by few pilgrims. Everyone works incredibly hard and hardly prays at all. The long-haired rabbis with their unkempt beards and black kaftans are almost an anachronism and have little religious influence on the young men of steel who are building Israel. The last of the prophets fled the country long ago, just as Jonah once boarded a ship at Joppa to flee from the command of the Lord.

Near this city of Joppa, now called Tel-Aviv, the airplane that brought me in ten hours from Brussels to Palestine via Frankfurt and Athens circled and landed one hot July night of 1957. Behind us lay the sea, deep blue by day, now like hammered silver in the moon-light. Far in the distance, lost to view, floated the islands we had passed over, fantastic animals with curved grey-brown backs full of wrinkles and clefts, rising menacingly from the water. Beneath us, the Holy Land, warm and firm under our feet, which, after a leap of a thousand miles, were getting accustomed to the earth again.

I had not come as a pilgrim any more than had my fellow-travellers. I could stay just five nights and four days—one hundred and four hours—in Israel. I did not go to Jerusalem and was able to visit only a few shrines. I was allowed to celebrate Mass in the cave dwelling at Nazareth where the Angel of the Lord spoke to Mary and where the Word became Flesh. Where the synagogue once stood, in the ochre-brown ruins of Capharnaum, I re-read in St. John's Gospel the Eucharistic promises that Jesus had spoken in that very place, to unbelieving people. I drank out of the hollow of my hand from the Lake of Genesareth, on whose sloping banks and rippling waters our Lord once walked. But only from a distance did I see the hill of the multiplication of the loaves and fishes and the Sermon on the Mount and Tabor, where Jesus was transfigured. This was all I could gather in passing, as a personal experience and blessed souvenir of Palestine.

For I had not come as a pilgrim, to follow the footsteps of the historical Christ. I had been summoned to this country to discover Christ suffering in our own time, to see how He is beaten and humiliated in hundreds of thousands of Arab refugees and in the eighteen thousand Arabic-speaking Catholics who dwell in the country of Jesus, the last remnant of a Christian country baptised by the Apostles. It was my task to find out how Aid to the Church in Need could lend consolation and relief to these poor brethren. At the request of the Archbishop of Haifa, the Cardinal of Malines had asked me to organise a relief movement on behalf of the refugees and the Arab Christians threatened in Galilee. Now I was journeying with Bishop Hakim back and forth through the scorched country. I visited our fellow-Christians in Haifa, Nazareth and Akko; I saw the ruins of the Catholic villages; I lived in the huts and tents of the Arab minority.

In the Near East there are four hundred and twenty thousand Arab refugees, victims of the conflict between Israel and the countries of the Arab Bloc. When, in 1948, after the revocation of the British Mandate, the Jewish inhabitants of Palestine proclaimed the State of Israel, the Arab population was left in a tragic dilemma. The radio stations of the surrounding Arab states broadcast: "Leave your dwellings, we will drive the Jews into the sea!" The new Israeli broadcasting stations urged the Arabs to remain. Most of them left their villages, with the firm hope of returning soon. It was a vain hope: unable to return, they had to remain in camps. There are ten thousand Arabs crowded together in each camp; thousands of camp children are born there every year. It is merely a matter of extending the barbed wire fencing; the military governors make sure that there is no revolution. In the land where Christ proclaimed the great law of love for one's neighbour live these poor uprooted masses for whom the law of love remains a dead letter. Those who stayed behind were often no better off. Their villages lay in the battle zone of the Arab-Israeli war: finally they too had to flee or be evacuated. Among them were many of the eighteen thousand Arab Catholics.

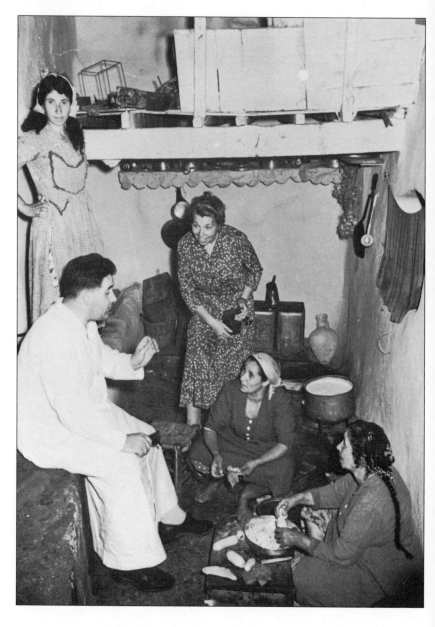

PLATE 25. Father Werenfried in 1956 with an Arab refugee family in Haifa. A major relief campaign followed.

There is no sense in discussing fault and responsibility in this part of the world. It is so natural that the suffering Jewish people should yearn for a homeland of their own. And it is so evident that the native population should resist the newcomers. Tension between young and old, between backwards inertia and a vital urge to progress, was inevitable. The ancestral population is now suddenly confronted with the materialism that the Jews brought from *our* pagan world. Abortion is officially recognised. Girls who lived like Mary in their villages have been forced by sheer poverty to find work in the cities, where they are ruined spiritually and morally in surroundings against which they have no defence. And the Israelis, surrounded on every side by the threat of the Arab states, are obliged by the instinct of self-preservation to be on their guard against the Arab minority in the land that they had bought from farmers and shepherds in order to find peace at last.

Indeed, I have a great sympathy for the perilous position of the Jewish people, for their efforts to form a unity out of the multitude who have returned, not from twelve tribes, but from a hundred nations: a unity of language and customs, one nation with one purpose. I can understand that these people, who have so seldom experienced mercy and goodness, are now unrelenting towards others and refuse to be retrained by feelings that seem to them sentimental. I did not come to judge the Jews, but to help the refugees and the oppressed.

One was Yussef, who died the night after I visited him. In the company of the *Doctora*, the woman doctor from Nijmegen who showed me around the area where she works so heroically, I was visiting the village of

Mizra. There are three hundred and sixty Arab refugees living here in huts made of sticks and corrugated iron; they have no jobs, and no means of support. A small boy came to take us to see a dying man. . . . Yussef lay wheezing on a pile of rags; he had been unconscious for two days.

Old Tamara, Yussef's wife, waved a withered bunch of straw over his yellow face, not to fan him, but to keep the flies from creeping into the open mouth, between the teeth and into the nose of the dying man. Tamara tells in a plaintive voice the story of what they have been through. The little Arab sister, Asma, who is accompanying us, translates a word here and there for *Doctora*. The latter listens patiently and examines the patient with such impressive tranquillity that we quite forget in what impossible circumstances she has to carry on her work. There is nothing more she can do. Her small hospital in Haifa is full to overflowing, and there is hardly ever room for an Arab in a Jewish hospital. Yussef is beyond help. The old woman asks me to say a prayer for the dying man. I say a Hail Mary in my own language to Our Lady of Flanders and give conditional absolution.

We leave the hut in silence.

That night Yussef died without recovering consciousness. Abuna Nicolas, the holy, white-bearded priest we fetched from another village, kept watch at his bedside with old Tamara until the full moon hung above Mount Hermon and Yussef's heart stopped beating. Thus Yussef died, of homesickness and misery, in the village of Mizra. He had once been the richest man in the district. Nine years ago young Israeli soldiers entered his village,

PLATE 26. On the ancient caravan route in Palestine.

Bassa, on the Lebanese frontier: the village had to be evacuated for ten days. After that, inhabitants might return to their primitive houses, to their fields and flocks. That is what the young Jewish lieutenant who led the troop said.

Ten days became nine years. Bassa was demolished and the land given to Jewish immigrants who set up a kibbutz on the other side of the road. There the people work feverishly to build up the new Israel—but Yussef died because of it.

There are many Yussefs in Israel. What happened in Bassa has happened in many places: I visited Hukrit and Malul, where the Jews left only the churches standing, and in Mujaidel I saw how the last traces of the Arab houses were cleared away by bulldozers. Here, too, the Orthodox and Catholic churches were left standing, for the government wishes to avoid any appearance of religious persecution. Near the place where the village stood are the wooden houses and huts for the Jews who are cultivating the land. In Galilee I saw six Catholic churches without a village and without a congregation; and the faithful are crowded together in *bidonvilles*, villages built of tin, without churches.

Here is the Church in need. In 1948, the archdiocese of Galilee had thirty-five thousand Arabic-speaking Catholics. In 1957 there were only eighteen thousand left—a small, fervent community, the direct descendants of the first Christians in this diocese of Jesus, Mary and Joseph. The Jewish and Roman persecution of the Christians, more than twelve hundred years of Moslem and

Turkish atrocities, the storm of the Crusades and the massacre of the Druses in 1860 were not able to destroy this Arab Christianity. The community stood firm, small in number, but strong in the Faith and morally pure. They were not modern: they remained true to their ancient customs and lived as Jesus Himself had lived in this small country marked by His footsteps. Eighteen thousand Catholics of the Eastern rite, pious Melkites of deep faith, living temples of Jesus Christ, infinitely more valuable than the stone shrines with which this faithless land is strewn, and where Turks, Greeks, Latins, Copts, Jews and Armenians have been fighting each other for centuries, for a couple of square yards of church floor space and the revenues of the sacred places. These sacred places attract tourists and foreign currency to Israel, and so they are protected and restored by the government. But if these last poor remnants of the Catholic Church in Palestine are not supported from abroad, they will perish. And, without living Christians, the most sacred places will have no further sense or significance.

As a result of my journey, eighteen thousand Christians experienced the charitable attention of the universal Church through the good offices of Aid to the Church in Need. Through a mass collection of material for recycling, we gathered the millions of dollars needed by the struggling Church in Israel. But for Yussef our help came too late.

HORROR IN ASIA

(1959)

In 1959 I visited the distressed areas of the Far East to find out what ACN could do for the refugees there. What I saw was so terrible that I shall never forget it as long as I live.

I visited Seoul and the desolate refugee areas of South Korea, where four million refugees from the Communist North have been given accommodation. There is no industry and no housing. The people are out of work, underfed and demoralised. I climbed the terrible Namsan Mountain, covered as with a crust with huts and hovels, small huts taking up a space of three hundred to three hundred and fifty cubic feet. They were thrown together out of paper, tin cans, cardboard, slats and pieces of canvas. There is no room for a man to stand upright. In each hut live five to ten North Korean refugees: they sleep on the floor winter and summer. They are malnourished and badly clothed. There are no toilets. The water has to be fetched from miles away in tin containers. There is no electricity. The cooking is done on an open fire—if there is anything to cook!

I stood in front of one of these hovels, so poor that the animal protection agencies would protest if it were used as a stable for a goat. In front of the door, two and a half feet high, were three pairs of shoes. As Koreans sleep on the floor (first pasting shiny paper on it), they take off their shoes before going in. Three pairs of shoes in front of a condemned goat shed! It seemed impossible to me that three people could live there. When I crept in, I found not three but *six* inmates. The other three had no shoes.

I also visited the ragpickers. There are seventy thousand of them in South Korea: boys who have run away from home, orphans and foundlings who have formed gangs of fifty to sixty under a chief. The older boys search the streets for waste paper and rags; the smaller boys beg food from the Americans or in the restaurants, or steal it to keep the gang from starving. I found fifty-seven of these boys in the coal cellar of a ruined factory. They are the lowest level of Korean society and are not looked upon as human beings—they have no papers or identity cards. In a corner of the coal cellar I saw a crucifix and holy pictures on the wall. Apparently some lay apostles had been in contact with these fellows. Twenty of them had already been baptised. These conversions had bitter consequences, however. Now they could not steal any more. The result was that they were living in still greater poverty than before, because they had become Catholics. The little beggar boys had been sent by their chief to an orphanage, so that they would not be in danger in the street and could at least learn to read and write. I promised help to these refugee boys.

Thank God that there is help at hand in Seoul. I met four brave women there. They belonged to the Women's Mission Aid, which has its headquarters in Brussels. One was Italian, another Korean, a third Canadian and the fourth German. They lived in the same poor and primitive way as the Koreans themselves. They slept on

PLATE 27. 1960: Father Werenfried in Seoul with Korean refugees
from the Communist north.

the floor in an old wooden house with no heating; half of this building had already fallen down. I celebrated Holy Mass in the attic, and when I knelt down the walls shook. The whole house was filled with girls, refugees from North Korea who had come by the thousands to Seoul to study.

There are seven universities in Seoul. But the students have no money and no work. They have nothing to eat but what is distributed by the Americans. Many girls, finding no other way out, sell themselves to American soldiers. This allows them to study, but it often ends in suicide. That is why these lay-helpers share their uninhabitable dwelling with dozens of Korean girls. Here, too, I promised in the name of Aid to the Church in Need to help build a new hostel for female students.

I was also in Hong Kong, beautifully situated behind a necklace of heavenly islands, the only door between China and the Free World. In this port without a hinterland there are one and a half million refugees. Since the end of the war the population has increased sixfold, and there is no room for these masses of people. The government does all it can to enlarge this small bridgehead of freedom; whole mountains are dug away and thrown into the sea to make room for houses. One concrete block after another shoots up on the newly-won land: each one seven storeys high, allowing nine and a half square yards for each family, with an average of eight persons per family. On each floor there are two lavatories and a tap. Four thousand people live in each concrete block; three hundred and fifty thousand have been accommodated in these drab mass dwellings. But think of all the poor little Chinese children who can only dream of flowers and animals!

Above the roofs of Hong Kong a new city has sprung up; three hundred thousand refugees have found a wretched roof over their heads under tarpaulins and in wooden huts on top of the flat roofs of the houses. Three hundred thousand more are housed in ancient junks, rowboats and rotting barges, where they live with the rats in stinking, brackish water. On the hill slopes, in caves and tunnels and amphitheatres of improvised huts, a further six hundred thousand refugees have found a desperate foothold.

In Saigon I encountered leprosy—two hundred thousand lepers, of whom only two thousand are receiving medical care. In the whole of South Vietnam there are only four hundred doctors for twenty million people. The sick people are hideous to see. . . . I saw a woman with her face eaten away, black holes instead of a mouth and nose. She was blind. She raised two small stumps of arms in my direction, and a hoarse croak came from her throat. I saw people creeping along on the remains of their hands and feet. One followed me, hopping on one leg, the whole time uttering the same incomprehensible sounds. A beautiful little girl of twelve with great, friendly eyes had one foot eaten away by leprosy. I saw great crowds of people disfigured by this terrible disease, unrecognisable lumps of flesh that might have been saved by one dollar—the small injections which can cure the disease in the initial stage cost only one dollar. But our mad world prefers to invest money in atom bombs, sputniks and jet planes and allows mankind, the king of creation, to whom God has entrusted the earth, to rot away on the dung-heaps of Asia.

Close to Saigon I visited "Freedom Village", where an old Chinaman called out to me: "I have no son and no daughter, so I have no rice. Without rice I cannot live, nor can I die!" He cackled insanely and waved his gin bottle. This village of freedom, where Chinese refugees are housed, is not a village at all, but one enormous barn. The ground is covered with mats of rice straw. Each mat is four square yards, and serves as bed, table and house for a whole family. Five feet higher up we get the second storey. On a floor of mouldy planks, more mats, the same scene. Another five feet: the third storey and then the fourth. . . . A thousand displaced Chinese in a gigantic barn with a leaking roof through which the monsoon drives the rain in sheets: human flotsam and jetsam that escaped the Red flood only to be stranded on the rocks of our lovelessness. Is it not our concern that millions of people should be deprived of the love of Christ in the darkest hours of their lives because we are callous and indifferent? If we do not bother about these desperate people ourselves, others will. And God will perhaps permit them to vent their wrath upon our tabernacles and quench the altar lamps in our churches. For why should Christ live in a steel safe if He cannot dwell in the hearts and lives of those who bear His name?

Then came Calcutta. A million homeless people live, sleep and die in the scorching streets of this metropolis. A hundred thousand others, mostly refugees from Pakistan, live on the pavements. They have built tiny huts,

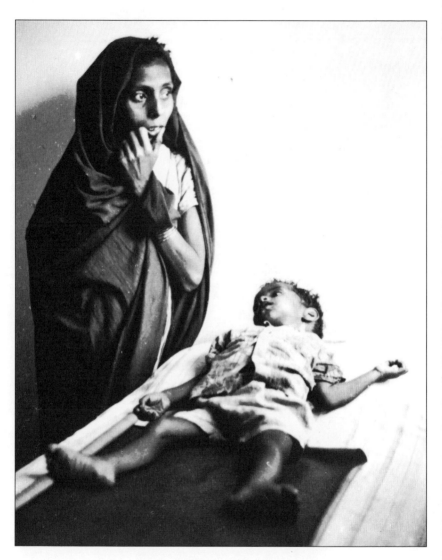

PLATE 28. "In Calcutta I baptised a dying child."

strung together for miles, leaning against the walls of the houses. The greatest height of their slanting roofs is four feet. Past these kennels flows the brown, muddy water of the gutters. There is no food and no work—nothing. Of the four hundred million Indians, three quarters are undernourished. Only the sacred cows are better off—it is said there are two hundred million of them. They wander unhindered through the streets, block the traffic, devour the contents of greengrocers' shops; they may not be chased away or killed. And the people are starving. There are homes for aged cows, but not for aged people.

The only one who is concerned about the people is Mother Teresa. She cares for the foundlings she fishes every morning out of the dustbins and for the sick and the dying. I visited her in the house for the dying. The house is quite near the Temple of Kali, and it used to serve for temple prostitution. Now it is a last home for lonely dying people. Above the door stand the words *Home for Dying Destitutes*. Mother Teresa's nuns and helpers go through the streets and look for the dying; they carry them on litters to their home. When I visited, there were one hundred and twenty-seven in that house: six long rows of litters next to each other. Withered skeletons lay and waited for death: dark feverish eyes stared at me. But Mother Teresa and her helpers stay with them, and, perhaps for the first time in their lives, these dying people experience selfless love. Mother Teresa is an Albanian nun from Yugoslavia who has lived for thirty-seven years in India. About fifteen years ago she founded a congregation for the purpose of looking after only the poorest and most destitute. There are already one hundred twenty-five nuns, of whom six are European.

There was a girl from Freiburg there. Four years ago I had preached in Freiburg, and after the sermon she had come to the parlour and told me she wanted to dedicate her life to God in the service of the very poorest, and could I tell her where to go? I honestly did not know. I promised that I would pray for light and advised her to discuss the matter with someone who knew her intimately: then God would certainly show her the way. I never heard anything more of her. But in Calcutta I recognised her in the house of the dying, and she recognised me. She had been working there for a year and a half. In the last few years they have been able to show a little love to more than twelve thousand dying persons. It is not so much the sari or the bowl of rice, but the motherly care that illumines their last days like a miracle.

In Calcutta I baptised a dying child in the arms of its sixteen-year-old Muslim mother—for I am not only a beggar, but first and foremost a priest, who is glad if he can baptise a child. Nobody noticed I gave the child the name Werenfried. Ten minutes later little Werenfried was dead. When the men came to take him away, I went with him. We arrived at a fenced-in place close to the Temple of Kali. There were seventeen trenches in the ground with wood fires burning in each one. For each corpse, forty rupees' worth of wood must be bought. Those who are rich buy a can of petrol as well—it takes less time. Without petrol it takes at least three hours. The child was laid with the other dead people on the ground until a trench was free. A man who had been run over by a tram had just been thrown on the fire.

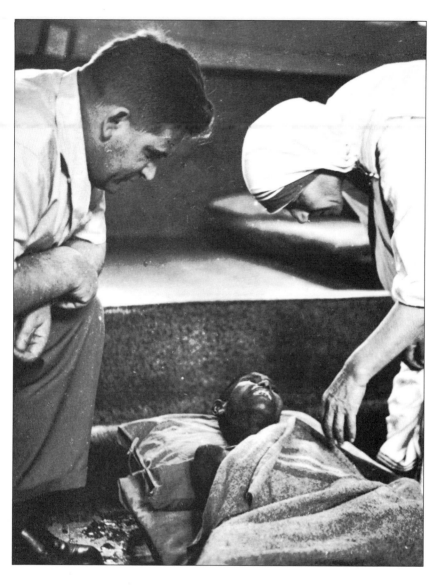

PLATE 29. Mother Teresa was caring for the orphans, the sick and the dying. Father Werenfried visited her in 1959 in the "Home for the Dying".

The relatives waited patiently and chatted with one another. Children were playing with bones that had escaped the fire. A sacred cow wandered among the burning trenches and snuffled at the dead child. From time to time there was a muffled bang: this was a skull exploding. Every time a body was ready, the ashes were gathered in a pot and thrown into the river ten yards further along, where children in the water were splashing and playing with mud and ashes.

In this macabre scene human beings are nothing more than a scrap of flesh, a piece of bone, a heap of ashes. Why are these people still so little affected by Christianity, after four centuries of contact with it? The reason is that we Christians have been criminally lacking in pure love and brotherly help. This is especially the case with the Christian peoples who, as colonising powers, have borne the responsibility for the development, the education and the religious instruction of the so-called underdeveloped countries. I know, of course, that we are not personally responsible for the sins of our fathers. But we are indeed responsible for furnishing the present-day charitable service which our dead ancestors of the colonial era can no longer supply.

I have been in places where the rats would die if they had no more to eat than the people do. I recall reading somewhere that there are areas where four hundred and fifty out of every thousand children die in their first year because they have nothing to eat. One hears of the parrots in New York being given elocution lessons by television, but there are today six hundred million children in the world without schools or teachers. They will remain illiterate all their lives. In certain regions half of the population dies before the age of fifteen. Two thirds of humanity is hungry. Tomorrow the dust cart will visit our houses to take the food we have thrown away, but in Calcutta the dust cart will come to clear away the corpses of those who have died of hunger during the night. If a dog is run over in these places, the children fight for a piece of flesh or a bone to put their teeth into. This is the harsh reality, and we cannot shut our eyes to it.

I have now been working for ACN for more than forty years. In these years I have seen terrible destitution and sorrow. But such things as these I had never experienced. I think it my duty to write this: I do not know how things can be improved. I only know that we must do everything—*everything*—and that our Organisation has a task here: for in one way or another this has to do with refugees or with the Church in need. For such things lead inevitably to religious persecution. And indeed the future of Communism—and, therefore, also of Christianity—will be decided in the countries I am writing about.

There is a tragic passage in Holy Scripture: "He came to His own, and His own received Him not!" There was no place for Him because "His own" were without love. This is the dark root of all wars and destruction, wrongs and disorder. Without Christ, everything goes wrong, because He is the Head governing the whole of mankind. And Christ is present only where there is love.

Let us therefore, in the name of God, restore love, which opens doors and hearts to Him. We human beings are one race. All of us. Even the most primitive peoples of the underdeveloped countries and the millions of starving people in our present-day world. The foundling in the dustbin and the weeping mother of little Werenfried, whom I baptised; the old Chinaman with his bottle of gin and the refugee on a barge in Hong Kong. The knowledge-hungry girls of Korea, who sleep with the Americans out of sheer poverty, and the little ragpickers who have stopped stealing: they all belong to us, and we to them. We must love each other and help each other. Like St. Martin: he was riding his horse; a beggar cried for help; but St. Martin had nothing left to give. So he took his cloak, cut it in half and gave one half to the beggar. Half, reader! The beggar was Christ. Every poor man is Christ!

WE JUMP OVER THE CURTAIN

In 1952, Aid to the Church in Need organised the second "Congress of the Church in Need" in Königstein. One hundred and fifty representatives from eighteen different nations reported on the state of the persecuted Church behind the Iron Curtain. They considered the possibilities of bringing relief and consolation both now and in the future to the martyrs of the modern Church.

The Congress was a high point in the history of our enterprise. A cardinal, five bishops, four abbots and several dignitaries from Eastern Europe took part in the discussions. The Holy Father sent us his special blessing. Many Western European bishops sent personal representatives. The chief religious orders were represented by their superiors, various organisations by their leaders, and Catholic learning by competent experts.

First there were well-documented reports on the gulf between East and West, a great panorama of the persecuted Church, and a clear exposition of the nature of the Communist philosophy of life.

Then came the witnesses of the suffering Church: Rumanians, Croatians, Czechs and Slovaks. They spoke about the atrocities, the spiritual and physical destruction which the Communists had caused. A Hungarian dignitary, a Polish prelate, a bearded Russian priest, a fiery Ukrainian: each spoke—sadly or passionately, according to their nature—about muzzled Shepherds and weakened flocks in their countries. It was a bitter and yet glorious reckoning. The no-man's-land between East and West, the Soviet zones of Germany and Austria, and the desolate refugee areas of Western Europe were once more surveyed. The bloodshed and lamentations of Albania and the Baltic states were heart-rending. A bishop exiled from China was the last in this sombre line of witnesses.

They were days of horrible alarm. Who would not be ashamed of the superficiality and indifference of a Western Europe that knew not a fraction of what was going on, just a day's journey from their doors? Which among those present did not swear to make every possible effort to open the eyes of the West and rouse it to action on behalf of this tragic struggle of sixty-three million persecuted Catholics?

Plans were made for the near and more remote future. ACN must become an international movement of love permanently in action to console the peoples of the East. An appeal would be made to Europe to send a great wave of prayer across the East. We would make new efforts to reduce the high mortality among the outcast and refugee priests of all nationalities. Through these priests the emigrated East European Churches would experience the charity of the Western European peoples. By building more spiritual bases—convents, churches and seminaries—Aid to the Church in Need would try to bring more tenacity, more strength to struggling Christianity in the no-man's-land between East and West, so that the full glory of Christ might be revealed to the starving East. We spoke for the first time of the foundation of the Building Companions, as an attempt to combat the housing shortage. A firm resolution was made to recruit legions of new priests from the ranks of European youths with the bold apostolic aim of re-Christianising Eastern Europe. They should be priests with an "Eastern heart" and with the soul of a missionary, ready—in God's good time, when He has opened once more the door to the East—to fill the spiritual vacuum of those afflicted countries.

This congress was a turning point for ACN. With the "economic miracle" in sight, we decided that, thenceforward, we should give precedence in our relief work to the non-German groups of displaced persons, rather than to those Germans driven from their homes abroad, whose problems were slowly but surely nearing their solution. Here we took a leap over the Iron Curtain, making a momentous decision to devote a part of our energies to the preparation of a better future for Eastern Europe.

The congress was a breakthrough for Catholicity. Here men from East and West met, prepared to break down the terrible chain reaction of blow and counter-blow, of eye for eye and tooth for tooth, prepared to grasp each other's hands in spite of all national differences, to annul hate and forget centuries of bloodshed and atrocities, and to become brothers once more in the supranational community of one Mother Church.

We all agreed that the climax of the congress was the moving hour of prayer that we offered up together for the nations of the persecuted Church. In eighteen languages, the tidal wave of prayer beat against the shore of God's eternity. The blood-stained parade of martyrs stormed Heaven again and again with their imploring *Parce Domine*. A cold shiver crept through the beseeching multitude when martyred Ukraine and suffering Russia, in the person of twenty of their sons, raised their voices in lamentations and tempestuous cries for help.

We left the place in dead silence, with the Cross of Christ standing out against the red, eastern sky—the Cross which is the sign of victory.

Deeply moved by all this, I meditated in those days on the attitude Christianity should adopt, and I wrote:

Autumn and winter are at the door: the days are growing shorter and the sky is darkening over a sombre world. The sighs of relief that rise in the world at every smile from a Communist dictator prove how heavily we are oppressed by an almost unbearable anxiety. Not only fear for our own lives and property, or for the future of our own children: but also, for some of us in our best hours, fear for the Kingdom of God.

God has suffered whole provinces of the Church to be overrun. One hundred eighty East European and Asian bishops have been incarcerated, exiled or murdered or have died without successor. Many thousands of priests and almost twice as many religious have been taken prisoner or driven away. There are tens of thousands of martyrs and hundreds of thousands of silent confessors in concentration camps behind the Iron Curtain; sixty million Catholics among Christ's sheep who have been delivered defenceless into the hands of their persecutors. And by the hundreds of millions can be counted immortal souls who by deceit, force, enticement, propaganda and the refined devilry of modern psychology have been converted to the pseudo-faith of a system that may be called an anti-Church.

Should we not therefore be inventive and self-sacrificing, even cunning, in our attempts to alleviate the blood-stained Way of the Cross of the persecuted

Church? If it were God's will that even Veronica's cloth should not be forgotten after two thousand years, should we not make every effort to support our suffering brothers and sisters by a sign from afar, by a glance of sympathy, by a word of encouragement, by a gesture of loving help?

It is God's Will that the blood-stained hemisphere lying to the east of our own should again become His Kingdom, and He thinks with endless longing of the millions that are no more of His fold.

And we, do we ever think with love and care of Asia and Russia, of the Communists deformed by colonial or despotic systems growing up in the cold shadow of a loveless world? Is it right for us to wish to destroy them because the sun of grace does not shine in their hearts? Ought we not, rather, to pray fervently that they may one day take Christianity much more seriously than *we* have done, we who have had the opportunity for so many centuries, and who have, for the most part, missed our opportunity? Even if they hate us we must save them: and this will only be possible by the power of the living Christ, who extends the hand of redemption and liberation to them through us.

The countries of the West are not eternal. All civilisations pass away. We may be living on the border of two civilisations, and it may be that the last task of present-day Christianity, on either side of the Iron Curtain, is to live and to die in such a manner that by our way of life and our prayers, by our love and our sacrifice, in persecution and in slavery, in prison and in death, the figure of Christ will be manifested in Holy Church in such a distinct and exalted way that the peoples of the future will be drawn to Him. That is why contact between the Church and the adherents of the Communist pseudo-religion is so important. During this contact, whether it is in freedom or in times of oppression, Christianity should be so active and living that the other side will be convinced of its truth.

This is the test that Christianity must undergo in the coming years. What the outcome will be is very hard to tell. The great danger lies in the possibility that, in our superficiality and false peace, we neglect to strengthen the spiritual defences of the Church: that we deprive our persecuted brethren of the spiritual, moral and material support they have a right to expect from us. We may also embitter our brethren in exile by our indifference and lack of charity if we fail to overcome, with goodness, the evil committed against so many, even here in the West.

In both East and West there are millions of our brothers who are victims of unjust systems, who are miserable, even desperate. These hopeless people are the battered vanguard of the Church. They must not only be made immune to the attractions of Communism, but so inspired with the sacred fire of grace and the Christian Faith that they are able to enkindle others.

ACN looks to the East and sees the dramatic struggle between Church and anti-Church already taking place. The persecuted Church and the Church in exile are calling out for help; and our Organisation is ready to help to the best of its ability by arousing, where it lies sleeping, the love that unites all peoples, the love by which we can be recognised as God's children.

Since then we have not ceased in our appeal to Christian people in Europe for spiritual and material help for the persecuted Church. For years, the attention of our Organisation has been focused behind the Iron Curtain.

PLATE 30. The Bacon Priest during the 1950s in the chapel–truck in which he crossed Germany, Austria, Switzerland and South Tirol begging for God.

On the occasion of the death of Stalin, during the uprisings in Berlin, Poland and Hungary and at the time of Tito's change of direction, Aid to the Church in Need took the initiative—mostly under a foreign flag—of transporting to the East, at lightning speed, enormous quantities of foodstuffs, books, medicine and other gifts of charity. Through continuous observation of the trade relationships between Eastern and Western Europe, we have become acquainted with all the trade agreements that are of importance for our purposes. We know from which countries consignments to which districts in the Eastern Bloc have the best chance of arriving. Our transport specialists are able to supply the majority of countries behind the Iron Curtain with gift packages, even though sometimes by circuitous routes. On my table in Tongerlo lie cheerless pictures of decayed and wrecked churches, with damaged roofs, shell-breached walls and broken windows, all behind the Iron Curtain. But I have also received photos of the same churches after they had been repaired with the loving help of our benefactors. So much was, and still is, possible. Economic conditions in the Soviet colonies of Eastern Europe are so bad that the Communist authorities are compelled to disavow their own principles for the sake of a little foreign currency. So, for the restoration of church buildings, it is possible to pay a sum of money—in dollars—into a foreign account with a guarantee that the equivalent amount in wood, stone, cement, iron and roof tiles will be placed at the disposal of our brethren behind the Iron Curtain.

In this way we have been able to finance the repairing of many sacred edifices belonging to the Silent Church. The frontiers of the majority of Red satellite states are still open, too, for theological books and breviaries.

Hardly a week passes without hundreds of books being sent to isolated priests, religious houses and seminarians. Of great importance is the provision of motor vehicles for the care of souls in Eastern Europe. And we have in our possession tens of thousands of addresses of large families who have received precious parcels of clothing from us. The number of persecuted Christians who have had personal experience of the consolation of Aid to the Church in Need runs into many hundreds of thousands. Even as far away as Siberia there are needy people who have received our help, albeit without knowing that our Organisation was responsible. Here are some statistics from a recent annual report:

> In the whole of Europe our warehouses worked at maximum capacity, preparing consignments for the Soviet Union, Poland, Czechoslovakia, Hungary, Yugoslavia, Eastern Germany and Rumania. Among other things these countries received: 21 cars, 89 motor-cycles, 10 bicycles, 1 printing press, 38 tons of paper, 4 film projectors, 5 typewriters, 11,498 different medical prescriptions, 19,860 clothing parcels, 100 tons of food-stuffs, 15,300 parcels of sweets, 8,793 theological manuals, 340 four-volume breviaries, 212 missals and 197 liturgical books, 500 tons of coal, 127 sets of vestments, 12 hearing aids, 2 organs, 1 truck, 3 tons of spare parts for automobiles and motorcycles, 1 tape recorder, 2 washing machines, 1 apparatus for baking altar-breads and 7 duplicators . . .

In the year 1963, Aid to the Church in Need provided a sum of 2,500,000 dollars for the campaign behind the Iron Curtain. In 1987 it was 14,448,000 dollars! In 1989 it was 18,140,000 dollars!

Much more important than this material help (about which, in fact, we can give very little information) is the spiritual help that the West must offer to the persecuted Church. This spiritual help should consist of prayers, sacrifices and repentance, according to the message sent to us by the Mother of God at Fatima and other places. Fatima is directly connected with the conversion of Russia. If no attention is paid to the message of Fatima, Russia will spread its errors and terror over the whole of the world; if, however, we do what Our Lady asked in Fatima, Russia will be converted. Only when Russia is converted can there be peace.

We do not know the "Third Secret". We do not know what races will be reduced to dust when the zero hour strikes. We are delivered up, to God's vengeance or to God's mercy. Terror creeps through the conference halls of the diplomats and through the anxious minds of nations. Tensely the Great Opponents stare at their radar screens, with trembling fingers stretched towards the fatal button: one touch, and the cringing earth will go up in flames. We do not know much: Lucia, the seer, has revealed only this much of the "Third Secret", that it will bring both pain and joy. We know neither the day nor the hour. But we do know that Our Lady meant simply to point out to us the warnings left by Our Lord Jesus Christ Himself in the Holy Gospel. For this reason it is high time that we at last take these exhortations to heart: that we should live pure lives, that we should do penance and be converted, and that we should pray the Rosary daily for the conversion of Russia.

ACN has organised impressive prayer campaigns for the persecuted Church and for Russia. For we know from Holy Scripture that the lonely, the poor and the weak, if they pray and do penance, are mightier than the powers of this world.

And why should not you, the reader of this book, be urged to take part in this way in the decisive conflict that is now being fought in the world? Think of the past: the walls of Jericho fell before the power of prayer, and Niniveh was spared because the whole nation did penance. The modern-day Jericho is the Kremlin, and we ourselves are the modern Niniveh that must be brought to repentance.

Say your Rosary daily. Pray for the conversion of Russia, for Communist leaders everywhere, for those who lead men astray and for those who have been led astray, for all who have become the willing tools of Satan. Do not pray only for the persecuted, but also for the hangmen who are in still greater spiritual need. Choose one of them. Make one of them your special target. Concentrate upon him the bombardment of your prayer and your love. Implore God, day and night, that through the intercession of Our Lady your Red protégé may repent and live.

Be a Good Samaritan. Pour the salve of your kindness and your prayers into the gaping wounds of malice. Offer your prayers and sacrifices from now on for at least one erring soul to find repentance and for one martyr to find the strength he needs. For even the martyr needs the strength not to throw down his cross out of terror, despair or rebellion in order to save his own life. In the vast regions behind the Iron Curtain, agony, the scourging, the crowning with thorns, the carrying of the Cross and the death of Jesus have again become reality. At the present time Jesus is mocked and humiliated, not in the court of Pilate, but in the great Siberian hospital where Archbishop Josef Slipyj, Metropolitan of Lviv, had to use his consecrated hands for eighteen years to clean filthy latrines. At the beginning of February 1963, he was banished to Rome, where, in 1984, aged ninety-two, he died in exile. Today Jesus was beaten to death in the person of the seventy-four-year-old Ukrainian Redemptorist bishop, Nicola Czarneckyj, Papal visitor for the Ruthenian Catholics, an old man with emaciated cheeks and sunken eyes wearily climbing the hill of Calvary with millions of other slaves bowed down not under a cross but under the burden of yet another five-year plan. It was the same with Cardinal Aloysius Stepinac, Archbishop of Zagreb, who died at last after fourteen years of imprisonment and internment in the village of Krasic, under the strict guard of a detachment of hand-picked Communists. The same story can be told of dozens of bishops, thousands of priests and nuns, of millions of Christians who are called to bear the Cross of Jesus somewhere behind the Iron Curtain through these darkest years of the twentieth century.

They are all tortured, ill-treated, bruised and trampled members of Jesus Christ. By your prayers and sacrifices you can adopt them, help them and console them spiritually, just as Veronica and Simon of Cyrene did on the way of the Cross in Jerusalem. Do not forsake them! Support them in their bitter need, so that they may persevere in faith and love and their blood may become the seed for a new and Christian Russia.

Reader, ponder seriously on this. Forget your little worries: listen to Our Lady, who induced us to write these lines. Cast from yourself all your pride and self-conceit: admit that there is no statesman, no general, no diplomat and no nuclear weapon able to save the world. Become a child once more, calling out for your Mother in mortal fear. Go to Mary! Be prepared to do what she has asked, even of you: pray the Rosary daily for the conversion of Russia with a boundless love that embraces both friend and foe. Repent of your sins and do penance: deny yourself a cigarette, a glass of wine, a visit to the cinema, deny yourself something that is, in truth, superfluous luxury. The money you save is no longer yours— give it to the persecuted Church through the intermediary of Aid to the Church in Need. We assure you we can turn it into effective relief.

Allow me, for God's sake, to make an appeal to you. I am not just a common beggar, but a priest who has discovered the weeping countenance of Christ behind the misery of these times. A priest who must fear to be judged and found wanting if he does not tell you the truth. And the truth is this: if you close your heart to your brother in distress, then God is not within you, because His love is not within you.

Once the Jewish people were menaced by powerful enemies. Day after day the giant Goliath appeared before the army of Israel, and challenged God's people with mockery and taunts. Terror filled the Jewish ranks, and nobody dared to meet the huge adversary—until the shepherd boy David went forth to attack the heavily-armoured giant with five small stones and a sling, trusting not in himself, but in the help of the Almighty. We know the outcome of the fight: those who fight on the side of God need fear nothing and no-one. What David accomplished with five stones and a sling, we can now attain according to the word of the Mother of God, with a Rosary, penance and repentance.

WITH GOD'S PARTISANS

It would be impossible to make plans and draw up relief programmes for the future of Eastern Europe without connections with the leaders of the persecuted Church. Aid to the Church in Need must not become the hobby of romantic dreamers. Our relief behind the Iron Curtain and our preparations for the "Day of Open Doors" must be guided by the most expert judges of the situation: the bishops and the underground bishops of the East. And since only a few of them are allowed to come to the West, we are obliged to go to the East. So now and again one of us has to risk his freedom and his life to hold essential discussions in the satellite States.

It is seldom that we can publish anything about these journeys: we do not want to put our friends in danger. On the other hand, we feel compelled to testify about the things we have seen and heard in Eastern Europe, especially since the ordinary tourist has no way of finding the real extent of religious persecution and is inclined to be under the impression that the Communist system has modified its anti-religious attitude. The increase of tourist travel in Eastern Europe thus acts as a soporific, a device used by the Communists to put the Western peoples off their guard, so that they will lower their defences against the great danger of Communism.

In 1959 I myself made an excursion through five "People's Republics", during which I visited many bishops and ecclesiastical authorities. I did not travel under my own name, and even the bishops I met did not know who I was. In every country I was accompanied by a trusted go-between who opened doors and hearts for me for a confidential talk. Without the guarantee of such a go-between, no bishop can take the risk of speaking his thoughts to an unknown foreigner. After due consideration, I have decided to recount my meetings with four bishops—suppressing, of course, the names of persons, places and countries and modifying the details somewhat. In this account I shall also give some particulars that I heard of during earlier meetings in Eastern Europe.

Before going into details, I should like to describe the general impression I received of ACN's work on the eastern side of the Iron Curtain. I was able to ascertain that our relief action, which amounts to millions of dollars, is both useful and necessary and generally attains its goal; the helping hand of our benefactors is present everywhere in Eastern Europe, wherever the need is greatest. I myself have ridden in some of the motor vehicles given in their hundreds by those who have heard my sermons, vehicles that have become an indispensable support for numerous bishops and priests. I have visited churches that have been resurrected from their ruins by the generosity of the friends of Aid to the Church in Need. I have witnessed the joy of a large family, when one of our gift parcels arrived by mail. I have shaken hands with seminarians who were able to follow their vocation thanks to an allowance from Aid to the Church in Need. But, most of all, I was able to ascertain, in dozens of personal conversations, how invaluable is the moral support and the consolation that these persecuted fellow Christians gain from our work.

It is to the everlasting merit of our benefactors throughout Europe that Aid to the Church in Need is again and again able to breach the Iron Curtain to break the spiritual blockade of the Church of Silence. God alone knows the number of those who were thus given the strength to remain faithful in this terrible affliction and to fight to the end!

I met the first bishop while I was visiting a cathedral. He looked like a peasant, kneeling before the tabernacle in his grandfather's black suit. The suit was worn out, too narrow in some places and too wide in others. There were patches on his trousers. My companion assured me that this was the bishop, although he wore neither ring nor pectoral cross. His diocese is marked by death, containing many depopulated villages with burnt-out houses and half-demolished churches. The people of these villages were murdered by the Communists or have emigrated to the cities. The parishes where there are still people are served by itinerant priests.

The bishop invited me for a trip on the back of his motorcycle to visit some churches under construction. A quarter of an hour later we were on our way. He had changed his clothes, and now wore a pair of brown corduroy trousers with black army boots, a roll-neck sweater and a dark grey raincoat. No purple.

We drove along appallingly bad roads to the first church: four walls without a roof, all charred black, and the altar standing under a wooden lean-to. The Blessed Sacrament and a couple of women in prayer were in a little room at the bottom of the steeple. Between these blackened walls Holy Mass is celebrated in the open air on Sundays: it is still a church, and there is a bylaw that says that a church may not be pulled down as long as it is still in use. So a priest comes here every Sunday to celebrate his third Mass. He is struggling to keep this ruin standing and has been trying for five years to get permission to build a new roof. He has not yet succeeded, but continues the paper war with tenacity. He may succeed—one day.

The bishop then took me to another village, where a church was being reconstructed. He climbed up the scaffolding and inspected the roof. He showed me with great pride the piles of cement bags, the old bricks, the wood and the great rolls of rusty iron reinforcement for concrete that he had collected for the building in the sheds and attics of tumbledown presbyteries.

He keeps up the struggle from one day to the next. His young priests, whom he calls by their Christian names, live in dire poverty. He discusses with them the technical and spiritual difficulties of their mission as church builders and pastors. For years he has gone on foot, by bicycle or by motorcycle from priest to priest to assist them, console, finance and encourage them. A battle has to be fought for every building permit, a battle that can last two years, six years, or even longer. If the building permit is granted, there are no building materials. If the building materials have been obtained, there is a struggle against the claws of the tax collectors threatening to confiscate everything to pay arrears in taxes. Then the building is begun, with feverish haste, often in the night by the pastor himself with his flock.

It is a spiritual guerrilla warfare with small defeats and victories; an underground fight, the only fight that is possible here. God's partisans, with this young partisan bishop as their head, are no longer afraid. None of them has joined the association of Peace Priests, the priests' syndicate that provides salary, pension and other material advantages. They have no income except what Providence puts into their hands from day to day. They are no richer or safer than the poor oppressed people in whose midst they were born. Many of them have suffered imprisonment, forced labour and torture for the Kingdom of God. Twenty priests of this diocese were murdered after the war, stabbed, shot, burnt to death or hanged. Their blood was the seed for new vocations. These young men have now become the best co-workers of their bishop.

I was with him until late at night. We viewed, by candlelight, another church that had been recently roofed in, and knelt before the humble tabernacle where Jesus lives among His persecuted brethren. The young pastor told us that the Communists had been so angry at the restoration of the church that they had even confiscated his bed and two chairs in payment of his tax arrears. With a smile he showed us the straw mattress on the ground which he sleeps on.

At the bishop's home—which consists of just *one* room—we talked for a long time. He rejected all compromise with the government, because he knows that every favour has to be paid for by a concession on the part of the Church, even if it be only a conciliatory silence with regard to some measures. "We cannot be dogs that do not bark", he said. His bright blue eyes shone in the lamplight when I left him at the dead of night.

The second bishop is dying on his feet. The patches on his worn cassock are covered by the shiny black overcoat he had wrapped himself in. His transparent face and thin hands bear the scars of the tortures he has been through. He has long ago left his bishop's palace and found accommodation on the second floor of his dilapidated seminary. It is one of the few seminaries in the country that has not yet been closed, and it is filled to overflowing with hundreds of seminarians, both boys and men from the surrounding dioceses that have lost their seminaries. The teachers look like labourers; they still have the calloused hands and weather-beaten faces that they had in the forced-labour camps from which they were released. The rector was in prison. The vice-rector was killed some years ago. The bishop is one of the uncompromising people who would not make peace with the Communist authorities. No one in his diocese has joined the organisation of Peace Priests. This explains why his clergy are the poorest I have ever met, without revenues, without fixed income and continually exposed to Communist vexations.

There are other regions where the bishops tolerate their priests' joining the priests' trade union; where the severe ecclesiastical sanctions with which those who joined were once punished are not now applied. There are even countries where a number of excellent priests joined these organisations on the secret instructions of their bishops to avert worse disasters, or where entire provinces of religious orders were inscribed by their provincials in the association of state priests.

This disastrous confusion is the fruit of Communist tactics of dividing the sheep from their shepherds and preventing contacts among the bishops and between them and Rome.

This bishop in his overcoat, however, had stood firm, as I had been told in many places. Yet he did not look like a fighter: he was small and old; the years of conflict with the powers-that-be and all the trouble brought upon his priests by his unyielding attitude had destroyed his health and wrecked his nerves. His hands trembled as he took me in silence to the library, where we could talk undisturbed: he was afraid that his own room might be bugged. The library betrayed the utter poverty of this seminary. It consisted of nothing more than a dusty collection of old-fashioned priests' books of the nineteenth century. Only three shelves of books by Noldin, Tanquerey and a few other authors were usable. There were twenty to thirty copies of each of these works: one manual for every four seminarians. None of them had their own textbook of dogmatic or moral theology. After their ordination, they go to their appointed parishes without books. Each new priest is given at least three parishes.

Many churches and presbyteries in this diocese have been destroyed. There was method in this destruction: flourishing Catholic provinces were demoralised and partly depopulated by mass murders, and the villages are peopled by outsiders, non-Catholics who owe their new life to Communism. In this way the power of the Church was broken.

In the dim light of the library the bishop unfolded a map; with short explanations he pointed out the most threatened areas. His thin hands glided over his diocese, sometimes with a gesture of loving protection and at

other times with a violent movement as if warding off
dangers. At one or two places of strategic importance,
his trembling fingers tapped decisively and emphatically
on the map. This small man, this bishop with an unvan-
quished spirit in his broken body, was God's strategist
in the spiritual guerrilla war behind the Iron Curtain.
He asked for help to reconstruct three centrally-situated
presbyteries from which three motorised curates (even
the motorcycles came from Aid to the Church in Need)
could serve the whole countryside. He is modest in his
requests. Perhaps each year a roof could be put on one
presbytery—the walls were still standing—and, for the
present, one small room made habitable. He did not ask
for much, but without our help nothing at all could be
done. The people were dying without priests to comfort
them. With tears in his eyes, he assured us that he would
gladly forgo all other aid if we could only help him with
this plan. I immediately promised him money and building materials for all three houses, although I had no idea
at the time of where I would get it.

This grey-haired old man is the head of a diocese of
martyrs. He showed me the obituaries of his murdered
priests, young men in the prime of their lives. He told
me how bravely his priests had spoken up before the
courts that condemned them. His soft voice trembled
as he told of the massacre of his people during the first
years after the war, of the deportations, of the lack of
understanding abroad as to the gravity of the situation,
of his sorrow at not being allowed by the government
to see the Holy Father for his *ad limina* visit and of his
fear that Rome might wish to come to a compromise
with Communism: "We cannot make a treaty with the
devil. We must follow faithfully in the footsteps of the

great martyr bishops, especially Cardinal Mindszenty and Cardinal Stepinac."

Then he invited us to see round the seminary: the bare chapel, the primitive refectory, the communal wash-room with nothing more than a row of taps over a piece of guttering. The dormitories were crammed full of rusty old iron bedsteads, rejects from hospitals and refugee camps. Twenty major seminarians slept in one open dormitory; for the junior seminarians there were fifty beds squeezed into one enormous room. The new priests slept six to a room; even the lecturers shared, two to a room. Not a single foot wasted: one square yard the less means one less vocation. There were no cupboards, only planks along the wall—running the whole length of the room. There were no chairs, no washstands. On the beds were worn-out straw pallets, lovingly patched and repaired by the nuns in plain clothes who looked after the housekeeping. On the walls there were a cross—and the compulsory portrait of the Red ruler of the country. "Christ died for him too", said the bishop with a smile.

In the daytime the seminarians lived in the gloomy halls where their courses are given. There were old-fashioned high desks on long legs with lids two feet wide: the entire living space of a seminarian for ten years while he is being trained for the priesthood. Downstairs was the basement, where the nuns lived and worked. Along the walls were numbered pigeonholes for the students' laundry; every Saturday a nun distributed clean clothes. But many pigeonholes remained empty because the students' parents were too poor—they were often

deprived of their livelihoods because their son was study-
ing at the seminary.

It is a miracle that there are still so many vocations.
Most of them are refused because of lack of space. For
some years the children have been allowed to enter only
when they are fifteen, after they have finished the athe-
istic state schools with their Communist educational
system. They have to interrupt their studies for their
military service, which often lasts three years. Almost
all of them persevere in their vocation.

The bishop knew the faults and shortcomings of the
past. He frankly admitted that the Church, with all its
privileges and earthly security, was in a state of spiritual
corruption. He could well understand that many older
priests did not have the inner strength to overcome the
present difficulties on account of their education and
traditions: "In the storm of persecution a whole epoch,
a whole generation has been lost. These young priests
of mine, who have been purified by fire and water, are
the only guarantee the Church has for the future in this
country."

These young priests, the best helpers of the little
bishop in his overcoat, are being trained by God Himself
in this working-class seminary. They are a legion of true
apostles, detached from all material wants and ready for
anything. They are amused at the measures that the
government invents to harass them. Even without our
aid they would persevere until the fall of Communism
or until their own death as martyrs. But we, on our
side, must fear the punishment of God if we leave these
bravest of the brave to their fate, if we are not prepared
to help them—whatever the cost.

The third bishop is seventy-three years old. Kindness shines from his thin, transparent face. He is extremely modest and courteous. He lives in an annexe of his dilapidated episcopal palace with three aged relations. He has no domestic staff. His day begins with an hour's meditation; then, at half past five, he celebrates Holy Mass. From seven o'clock (after breakfast: consisting of water and dry bread), he works at his desk; he has no secretary. Almost every Sunday he is off to administer Confirmation in the villages. He has no car: unaccompanied, he walks for hours through the deserted lanes of his diocese, uphill and downhill, in scorching heat, through rain and snow, to preach, to confirm and to encourage his poor priests and people. His priests live on the alms of their parishioners. But the bishop has no parishioners of his own, so that he is the poorest of them all.

This bishop stood before me with tears in his eyes. He, too, was concerned about the continued survival of his seminary, for which he had no revenues at all. He would very soon need really large-scale financial help. Hesitatingly, he mentioned the sum of twenty thousand dollars. Otherwise he would be forced to close the seminary.

The seminarians have no food, and the people can no longer help: they have reached the very limit of their capabilities. The buildings are on the point of collapse. There are no sheets or blankets. There is one glass for every two seminarians. There are no dinner plates—they have to eat from old food tins. Hunger and disease threaten the vocations of ninety-three seminarians. Many parishes no longer have a priest, so the Church cannot do without these vocations.

PLATE 31. After the war these barracks were turned into the seminary and "home" for the exiles. This institution in Königstein was the first major project of our Organisation. The seminary produced 465 priests. Since 1975, the international headquarters of Aid to the Church in Need has been based here.

The seminarians themselves are ready for any sacrifice. In this country, too, they have to do years of hard military service after their schooling. The bishop considers it a special grace of the Mother of God that not a single one of his students has as yet lost his vocation, and that all of them returned from the army unscathed spiritually and morally. The Holy Spirit compensates with exceptional gifts of grace for whatever the souls are deprived of by religious persecution. The parents of the seminarians, too, are heroic in their readiness to make sacrifices. The number of vocations has more than doubled in the last few years.

There is now less open persecution, but by means of economic pressure, loss of livelihood, the prohibition of church collections, unjust taxation and starvation, the government endeavours to undermine the loyalty of the faithful and the constancy of the priests. Help can only come from abroad. It would be a calamity for the Church and a disgrace for the West if God's work in the souls of these seminarians were allowed to be destroyed because Christians in the Free World withheld the help that was so absolutely necessary.

The fourth bishop uttered a warning against the dangerous temptation to search for a compromise between Church and Communism. As yet not a single Communist government—not even in Poland or Yugoslavia—has shown itself ready for a genuine coexistence with the Church.

For the Church behind the Iron Curtain there can be no *modus vivendi* with Communism, only a *modus moriendi*, a long but certain death-struggle in the grasp of a system that is in its deepest being materialistic, godless and diabolic. There is no point in trying to placate the authorities with concessions or with a slavish 'legality' to prove that the Church is prepared to adjust herself to the new conditions. The spirit and the letter of all Communist laws are in their very essence aimed at the destruction of the Church. If the Church obeys these laws, she is signing her own death warrant.

It is useless to try to conceal the fact that the Church in many countries of central Europe has been affected by a certain decay. Liberalism and Josephinism struck deep wounds, especially in the former Austro-Hungarian Empire; the material security offered to the State Church was not always conducive to the spirit of independence with which bishops and priests ought to resist abuses. For those working in Aid to the Church in Need's chapel-truck mission among the refugees from those countries, it has become clear how inadequate was the pastoral care in many of the countries that are now satellite states.

It is easy to understand, then, that some of the clergy and the great mass of the population were not able to stand up to the persecution of the Church, and that there are also bishops who only hesitatingly follow the defiant example of Cardinal Mindszenty and Cardinal Stepinac. The tragedy of the unfortunate Peace Priests, who served with the Communist regime mostly from fear, or for material gain, or to prevent worse things happening, was a proof of the confusion reigning behind the Iron Curtain.

It is not for us, from our safe position of liberty, to throw stones at those struggling with God, with their conscience and with their own human fears, and who do not always have the strength to choose the most heroic path. They are partly the victims of their upbringing and of circumstances over which they have no control. If we can ever apply Jesus' command not to judge, it is here. We must pray for them and think of them only with love. And we may ask ourselves whether *we* would be prepared to sacrifice everything for our Christian convictions. But we must never allow ourselves to be influenced by the compromise that they have made. And it would be dangerous to allow ourselves to be tempted in the name of "legality", as they do, to consider the steadfast resistance of the Church behind the Iron Curtain as wrong and exaggerated.

There are countries in Eastern Europe where eighty or ninety percent of church collections and donations must be made over to the State as taxation. There are countries where bishops and priests owe millions to the tax authorities, and where time and again sums of money, chairs and cupboards, typewriters or motorcycles are confiscated to pay these debts. Legality at all costs in such countries would be suicide for the Church.

In various "show-trials", bishops and cardinals have been condemned for having irregularly accepted financial support from abroad—this was called "violation of currency control regulations". The West was dismayed every time a bishop, accused of this crime, admitted his guilt. Afterwards this admission was an invitation to throw mud at martyrs and confessors, representing them as reactionary and political-minded clerics, and besmirching the purity of their spiritual conflict. This fate was not even spared Cardinals Mindszenty and Stepinac.

They were called fools because they ignored regulations that infringed the rights of the Church; they were disavowed by Catholics claiming to practice "pure" Christianity; but the oppressed peoples of the East are grateful to them for the risks they dared to take. And more than three years after the death of Cardinal Stepinac his tomb in the cathedral of Zagreb, still covered in flowers, is surrounded all day and deep into the night by throngs of praying people who, in his example, find strength not to betray God and the Church.

The Church is involved in a life-or-death struggle: legality, in the Communist sense of the word, can never become the guiding principle of her actions. Her new heroes and saints, who are prepared to obey God rather than men, are growing to full stature in persecution; they act according to their consciences and are ready to bear the consequences of their actions. Of course there are victims, but life must go on. And so we express our confidence and respect for the bishops, priests and laymen who, in dungeons and concentration camps behind the Iron Curtain, are atoning for "illegal" acts; we cry shame that heroes condemned by a sham justice in the East should be *disapproved of* by some Catholic circles in our safe West for not respecting the arbitrary and unjust laws of the Red reign of terror. This is why Aid to the Church in Need is vigorously seeking ever-new ways and means of bringing Western aid primarily to the tough, unyielding fighters who risk their livelihood, their freedom and their lives so that the Church in the East may survive the Communist terror.

THE SONG FROM
THE FIERY FURNACE

Only a few can risk the leap over the Iron Curtain to see how Jesus suffers in His persecuted Church. The love of many, roused by Aid to the Church in Need, can, however, penetrate throughout the East. And the echo of this love returns in thousands of letters, which reach us from all the countries under Communist oppression.

The Christians living through the terror of the dictators are like the young men of the Book of Daniel, Shadrach, Meshach and Abednego, who were thrown by Nebuchadnezzar into the fiery furnace. They are being purified for a future, but do not know whether they will see it on earth or in Heaven. They are being tried in their faith. The servants of the great tyrant do not cease, like the Chaldeans of old in the plain of Dura in the province of Babylon, "to heat the furnace with naphtha, pitch, tow and brushwood so that the flame shall rise nine and forty cubits above the furnace". But even now it happens that the martyrs walk through the flames praising God and blessing the Lord, and that an angel of the Lord descends to them so that the fire no longer hurts or scathes them.

The song of the persecuted Church in the fiery furnace of Communism has been recorded in countless letters, of which we publish here a number of fragments. A song crying to Heaven and overflowing with terror and distress, sorrow, hunger, pain and desperation. But sometimes we can observe that the angel of consolation has visited our tortured brethren. Know from this that Aid to the Church in Need was with them in your name.

A priest in East Germany writes:

My warmest thanks for the many parcels that I received from you through the intermediary of Mrs. K. There were many lovely things to eat in them, which I distributed to our old people. As they are no longer able to work they receive only a B ration card, which is not enough to keep a man alive. They are as pleased as children with every little gift that enlivens their menu. With great joy I also received the splendid purple vestments, the breviary with the new translation of the Psalms and the fine black material that I can make into a cassock. I feel a great debt of gratitude and will pay this debt as well as I can with my prayers.

A girl in Lithuania:

Dear Father, I begin with the words "Praised be Jesus Christ". With grateful hearts and eyes full of joyful tears we opened the parcel you sent us. Neither I nor my parents know what words we can use to thank you: my parents are in great need, and the parcel saved us. We shall never forget to pray for you every evening and close, with Christian greetings, Renata Woitias.

A young woman:

Yesterday we received the two parcels of baby clothes. There are moments when the words "thank you" are not enough to express one's feelings. . . . I cried, not out of self-pity as I often used to do, but because I was happy for the first time in many years. My husband returned from prison eight months ago, broken in body and spirit; I myself was in prison for seven years—but I shall not go on about my troubles. My father, who was the manager of a large bank, was given the opportunity, after forty-two years' service, to begin again as an ordinary clerk. All his property was confiscated. We are expecting a baby. We own nothing, and people who mean well say it was a crime to allow the child to be born. But my husband said: "If God grants us this child it is because He already knows how He will help us to make a good person of him." And that is what happened.

A seminarian in the East:

Although your parcel had only the initials T. W., I am sure I am sending my letter of thanks to the right address. I was overjoyed with the fine breviary—I am now one of the few in our seminary who possesses a breviary with the new translation of the Psalms, and I thank you from the bottom of my heart. I shall pray for you. I am going to be ordained in a fortnight. It will be the beginning of a difficult time for me, but God will come to my help.

A Rumanian bishop on the eve of his arrest:

The hour of Christian heroism has struck in our country. Our ancestors look down on us and say: "We gained our national liberty with blood and suffering. Now it is up to you to build the cathedral of liberty and of religious freedom of conscience." The Rumanian Catholic Church, the true Church of the Saviour among the Rumanians, is being persecuted. Jesus Himself, in His Mystical Body, is again being insulted, crowned with thorns and crucified. Many are leaving the battlefield and are afraid of Good Friday; yet it is now, precisely, that the time has come to profess the Faith without fear.

Providence is giving us the unique opportunity to win holiness through heroism, and we cannot refuse God and our homeland this glory. After almost two thousand years, it is our turn: the world has its eyes fixed upon us.

A Czech monsignor:

After having been taken prisoner and condemned to death for a trivial "crime" by the Gestapo, I was liberated by the end of the war. In 1948 one of my friends was arrested by the Communists and, after they had knocked out all his teeth and broken his hand, he signed a false testimony against me. I was taken before a people's court, and my sentence consisted of two years' imprisonment, confiscation of property and loss of all my rights. I was sixty-eight at the time, and I knew I would not survive. So I risked fleeing. One night I swam across the river that lay between me and freedom and crossed the Bavarian frontier two days later, soaked to the skin. I receive a pension of 85 marks a month. There is little that I can do as I am old and in ill-health, but I visit old and sick refugees who have become my companions in misfortune. Your parcels are very welcome, as they enable me to save something for my poor people.

A young Pole in Western Europe:

I lost my parents fifteen years ago. I was born in Eastern Poland. In October 1939, when I was fourteen years old, I was deported to Russia. I had to do very heavy work in a peat clearing near Smolensk. When the treaty with England, Russia and America was signed in 1942, we were taken to England; six months later I was at the front. . . .

There I found my brother, who had fled to England in 1939. To my sorrow, shortly afterwards he was shot down over Monte Cassino and was killed. Then I was again alone until the end of the war. The Polish soldiers had a terrible time. We were always fighting where the fighting was heaviest, and never for our own country. Because my brother and I were in the British army, my father was taken prisoner by the Gestapo in 1943. He died in Dachau on 7th April 1944, and was burnt in the crematorium. It might have been better for me too if God had taken me to Him. I have been searching in vain for my mother and another brother and sister—I don't know if they are still alive. They were probably taken prisoner by the Russians because we were fighting in General Anders' army and did not return to Poland. Now I am quite alone here in the West. I have no work, no relations or friends, not even a roof over my head. I sold my clothes for a piece of bread to keep myself from starving.

A family in East Germany:

We were delighted to receive your parcel—our heartiest thanks for everything. Every time a parcel arrives, we know that we have not been forgotten here. Our parish priest and curate have sixty-nine villages to serve. Their lives are often harder than that of a missionary in the jungle. It often happens that we have to go miles away to church to hear Mass on Sundays. In winter, when the roads are snow-bound, we remain in our village and pray together the prayers of the Mass. This year we celebrated Easter in a barn, half of which has been converted to a church. But the Saviour was born in a stable, and so we think that He feels at home with us.

The mother of a family in Šopron:

The parcel you sent us got through customs without any problems. It was a godsend to us in our bitter need.

My husband suffers from tuberculosis of the lungs and eyes and cannot work. So we receive only a category three ration card, which is not enough to keep us alive. But now we can keep going for a while, and it reminds us of the words of the Gospel: "Take no thought what you shall eat. . . ".

From a Communist encyclopedia:

The Vatican is the religious, administrative centre of the Catholic Church. It has always been one of the centres of international reaction. Today the Vatican is an active champion of the imperialist politics of the USA and Great Britain. It serves the criminal purposes of the American and English imperialists and of the firebrands of the new war. It is an irreconcilable enemy of the national freedom movement of the oppressed peoples and an agency of the imperialist conquerors in the colonial and dependent countries. The Vatican supports fascism and wages a bitter war against the USSR and the People's Democracies of the whole world.

A priest in East Germany:

I can hardly believe that the new Volkswagen standing before the door is for me and that I need no longer ride my old bicycle through all kinds of weather to bring the Last Sacraments to a dying man or to celebrate four Masses every Sunday in remote places. The person who brought me the Volkswagen will tell you how incredulous I looked when he told me I could keep the car. It seemed impossible to me that there could still be people capable of such great sacrifices for the extension of God's Kingdom. So I ask you to forgive me for my lack of faith.

A priest in Eastern Europe:

With joy I received your princely gift for our little church. Although I can say nothing to my parishioners about your noble deed, I have still found a way to thank you: every day after Holy Mass we say a prayer for the intention of an unknown benefactor. I enclose two snapshots of our church. The whole congregation, from the schoolboys to the engineer and architect, helped to build it.

A mother in Poland:

The parcel arrived on 19th March, my daughter Jozefa's nameday. She was born on the 19th of March, and that's why we called her Jozefa. My child was delighted. She thought it was certainly her daddy in Heaven who inspired you to help us on this very day. I also thanked God for sending us this pleasure—He has not forsaken us in our need.

A priest in Hungary:

You would not believe what a lot of good we can do with the parcels. We priests are not only the spiritual fathers, but also for a great part the foster fathers of our flocks; the people come to us with complete confidence. I received a letter from a schoolmaster to whom I regularly send a part of your gift parcels, saying that his children talk about nothing but the mysterious uncle who sends them parcels from a far country, because he knows they are poor.

A mother who visited her son, a priest, in East Germany:

I visited my son's parish with him. There is the same misery everywhere. The people come to the temporary churches from great distances, and these buildings are often in such a pitiable state that it is difficult to celebrate Mass there in a dignified manner; and yet these afflicted people pray in their wretched surroundings with an attention and fervour that is sometimes hard to find in our beautiful churches. After Holy Mass the poor come to the priest with their cares and troubles. He helps them as much as he can. The old people, especially, live in an indescribable state of poverty; as they are no longer able to work, they receive a ration card that gives them the right to very little food. If they do not want to die of starvation, they are forced to try to buy something without coupons. This gets them into debt, which they are afterwards unable to repay. In these cases the priest sometimes has real rescue work to do. The packages of nourishing food from ACN that I send on every month have already done a lot of good here.

A Slovakian priest:

I come from a prison in Slovakia where I was interned in 1945. In 1946 I was condemned to death, but two years later the death penalty was remitted to thirty years' imprisonment. After ten years' hard labour I was set free and had to leave the country immediately. Once in the West it is soon forgotten that there are still so many clergy and laymen in prison behind the Iron Curtain. We priests were kept strictly isolated from the lay prisoners. Among us were many bishops and higher clergy. We could say Mass only in secret: if the jailer discovered it we were severely punished. We learned a lot about the persecution from a bishop who was sent to prison in 1953: he told us that every priest who remains openly loyal to Rome ends up in prison sooner or later. Communication with the Vatican is considered high treason and espionage. Those members of the clergy who are willing to adjust themselves to the commands of the State may exercise a certain amount of sacerdotal activity, but they are closely watched by the State Department for Church Affairs. Actually, this Communist department more or less controls the Catholic Church in Czechoslovakia. Having myself lived for ten years in this atmosphere, I appreciate greatly everything you are doing for our poor brothers in the Faith in my country. I myself need nothing, as I have learned in prison to be satisfied with very little.

A parish priest in Hungary:

The five hundred catechisms have just arrived. You cannot imagine what help they are to me. Previously, the children had to make do with four different editions. For every seven children I had one catechism, which was sometimes copied by hand. Now I can give each child a catechism when he is confirmed. May God bless you.

A young man in Czechoslovakia:

My friend received a parcel, and he shared it with me like a brother. We both wanted to become doctors, but as we are not party members, we are not allowed to study. Now we are both working on a road-construction team. My health is poor, and I do not know how long I can keep up this heavy labour. I enclose my own address and that of a priest who works on our night shift.

A priest behind the Iron Curtain:

Dear Father, as founder of the chapel-truck mission, it will interest you to know that I have followed your example. With the help of some young working men I have rebuilt an old furniture van into a travelling church.

It is pulled by a borrowed horse for which we do not need a permit, and it does service as a chapel and catechism classroom in five localities. A colleague for whom I was able to get another removal van has followed my example, and we are going to rebuild two more vans for the same purpose. Fitting out the first one cost three hundred dollars: we hope to get the other one ready for a third of the amount. Do you know a good person who can spare a hundred dollars for this purpose? The channels are well known to you.

A father of a family in East Germany:

I used to be a judge; but now I work in a coal mine—you will understand why. My wife and four children live in poverty two hundred miles away. My wife earns some money as a charwoman; my children are not allowed to study. We cannot bear it much longer. The parcels you have been sending regularly to my family for so long are a great comfort to me.

A working woman in Hungary:

Maybe you have forgotten our revolution. We have not. I certainly have not, dear Father, for every time I think of my eldest son, János, who was crushed by a Russian tank, my mother's heart begins a new revolution . . . against everything. And sometimes—I have to tell you, Father—sometimes my heart revolts against God. Then I wonder . . . why? In the West they live in freedom and without care. For them Hungary is a long way off. They did not know János. But I did, dear Father, he was my eldest. . . . And then I received the parcel and the letter among the clothes. And now I feel again that they are thinking of us in the West; this has helped me very much. I have given the gray suit with the black stripes, which would have fit János so well, to my sister's son—they are worse off than we are. He was so pleased with the suit, but tears came to my eyes and I thought, János did not die for nothing. . . . Think of us, dear Father.

A nun in Croatia:

Your parcel has arrived safely. You have sent us everything we asked for! We have here an old, blind Sister who prays all day to thank you for your kindness. Your parcels made it possible for us to help poor children, and they will also pray for you. They have to put up with a great deal of ridicule and persecution because they come to church. Of the sixty children the reverend father prepared for their first Holy Communion, only thirteen arrived, without their parents. Everyone is afraid.

A priest in Albania:

Your parcels are a great comfort to me. I ask for your prayers that our courage may not fail and our faith remain strong. Often we have the impression of vainly defending a fallen outpost with the cry of agony on our lips: "Lord, save us, for we perish." The answer "Fear not!" came today with your parcel. Now we know that the Lord is faithful to us and will save us.

A grandmother in Hungary:

They shot Tibor, too. At six in the morning, pale as death, he was taken to the place of execution. I see his young face before me day and night. He was only fifteen at the time of the revolution, so they waited till he was eighteen so that they could shoot him. They knew very well that he was a worthy son of his father, and that he would never yield to them. Now the Communists have taken away the last thing that had any meaning in my life. Pray that God may come for me soon, so that I may see Tibor and all my dear ones again in Heaven.

The mother of a Czech priest:

We received a hundred and fifty coupons from Switzerland. We can repay your kindness only with our prayers. Just imagine: now that we have the coupons we can even get cement. You will perhaps laugh, dear Father Werenfried, cement is so ordinary! But our tumbledown house needs repairs so badly, and we have been trying for two years to get the cement we needed. With the coupons this will be very simple.

A priest in Poland:

My church is ready. Day and night my parishioners, simple working people, have been working to get the church roof finished. We owe the bricks, cement and iron to your kindness. I did not ask for a building permit, but when the supervising commission came with the order to pull down the church again, my workers marched up to them in a group. Courage is what is needed here. Those who are afraid are arrested, to break their spirit. Those who dare are usually shot—but at the moment this does not fit in with their plans. And so we can go on with the work.

A deported nun in Russia:

Dear Mother! At last I have a chance to send you a sign of life. Will this letter reach you? Or do you think me dead? It has been so long since we were taken to Russia. But don't you feel how my homesickness and

my longing beat at your door? How often have I cried:
"Don't forget us. Pray for us. Help us! We are so poor,
so forsaken, in the deepest misery. Don't forget us. Pray
for us!"

The things that we have to endure are very terrible.
We are treated like animals, driven to work with blows.
In fact, we are less than animals, for no one cares about
us. Whether we collapse and die on the spot or one of
the guards beats us to death, makes no difference. If
work does not go fast enough or if the guard is in a bad
temper, we are lashed with whips. First of all we helped
to build a large bridge across the Dnieper, heavy work,
man's work. We had to drag steel girders and push them
forward high above the wide river. Those who collapsed
were flogged. Those who did not get up were kicked
into the water by the guards. Many of our sisters died
there, and we envy them. Now we are working in a
mine, underground the whole day, in a choking atmosphere. Many have died there already.

If we only had somebody to encourage us, to support
us, to give us a little help! But we have nobody. We are
quite forsaken and isolated. No Sunday, no feasts, no
Communion. Only work, hunger, blows, a bare barracks, a hard wooden bed, and we ourselves clothed in
rags; always the hardest work and unsatisfied hunger.
We are hardly human any more.

We do our best to preserve our faith in God's Providence and to pray again and again: I believe, I trust. But
it is so dark in the soul, so very dark. Our souls cry
out: "My God, my God, why have you forsaken us?"
It is too hard to have no hope, no spark of light. Mother,
do you understand me when I ask: "How can God permit
this? Why must all this happen? How much longer will
it last? We shall all perish."

But we trust in His Providence. In spite of everything, we all still wear the cross on our breasts, and in the midst of all distress and desolation we take refuge in Him to Whom we shall be faithful unto death. But pray for us, oh, pray for us!

I cannot tell you everything, how they humiliate us, how they dishonour and spurn us. Yet we are all of us religious who have given our lives to Jesus and who, in spite of everything, belong only to Him.

But our distress, the distress in our souls—I cannot express it. We have no rights, we are at the mercy of everyone. Oh, those nights in which, in spite of our weariness, we are not allowed to sleep, in which we cry—and death is still waiting and does not deliver us.

Oh, mother, I do not want to burden you, I shall tell you only the least part. . . . May the Heavenly Father in His mercy look down upon us poor, outcast, violated nuns, who, in face of all this, still believe in Him, love Him and persevere for His sake in this endless dying.

Now I have made it difficult for you, dear Mother. I long only for one thing, that you pray much for us, so that we may bear all this suffering in union with Jesus' Passion and Death. Pray for us. Till we meet again in Heaven.

THE WAREHOUSE

The warehouse lies in the shadow of the abbey. The white Canons and the grey Brothers, the pigs and the cows, the green meadow and the pine wood and the solemn chimes that ring from the tower seven times a day—all these things belong to the abbey.

Having come here in 1934 to receive the habit and the name of Werenfried, I too belong to the abbey. I am grateful for the confidence it has had in me. For without the blessing of my abbot I could not have left the grey abbey gateway to go on my pilgrimage through the wide world, with the sound of the bells in my ears and the chanting of my fellow monks in my heart, in search of distress.

Aid to the Church in Need grew under the blessing of Abbot Stalmans, which was the blessing of God. Its office moved out of my inaccessible monastic cell to a room in the retreat house. A second room was annexed and a third followed, which was just about as far as the Tongerlo retreat house could go.

But ACN kept on growing. Into the three rooms we put more cupboards, more tables and chairs, more type-writers and telephones, and more staff. The work over-flowed through doors and windows. This was the case in Tongerlo, and it was the same in Antwerp. The warehouse moved from the Korte Sint-Annastraat to the Van de Wervestraat. Then to the Avenue d'Italie,

and from there to the basements of the St. Norbert
Institute, which some called the "catacombs of charity",
then to Avenue America, to Brussels Street, to Pecher
Street. . . . Aid to the Church in Need grew, and everything became too small. Then came the warehouse, in
the shadow of the abbey with the white Canons and the
grey Brothers, the pigs and the cows, the green meadow
and the pine wood and, seven times a day, the chimes
descending from the high steeple.

The warehouse is the headquarters and the pride of
Aid to the Church in Need. It was already in use before
it existed. First of all the high mound of gift parcels was
piled up in the open air under a tarpaulin. Around this
were built the walls of the warehouse. The roof had to
be three feet higher than had been originally planned,
because the bales of wastepaper for the salvage service
were piled up higher than had been expected. And in
some places the floor could not be cemented until a year
later, because it could not be cleared.

The warehouse grows and thrives as ACN does. It
keeps changing. It performs miracles with its cubic
capacity and finds a space for each new enterprise. It
contains rags and volunteers, foodstuffs and secretaries,
card indexes and lavatories, clothes and cars, dormitories
and shoes, jewelery and machinery. In its wide halls
there are real huts on stilts built for the staff, dormitories
for volunteers, a kitchen, a canteen, seventeen offices,
five special depots, showers and wash basins, a hall for
the permanent exhibition, a huge cold-storage plant, an
altar for Mass, a garage and a repair shop for motor
vehicles. Bold concrete constructions and dizzying

staircases make use of all the space available, right up to the last cubic foot under the roof.

Away down in the halls we can see a mountainous landscape of gift parcels and secondhand material. Here the helpers sweat and labour, having come from the whole of Europe at the summons of Aid to the Church in Need; here they sort and pack, drag and squeeze, load and unload goods for the Church in distress. Here the floors groan under the burden of charity. Here the spirit of Aid to the Church in Need moves like the wind, young and fervent as nowhere else. The warehouse is a story of talent, imagination, zeal, generosity, improvisation and organisation.

This is the place where volunteer and paid assistants deal with the huge quantities of material poured into the warehouse in a never-ending stream by the charity of Flanders, and which must quickly be sent on to the East. If necessary, work goes on here day and night on a three-shift system to empty the warehouse. But at the same time the collection and transport service is working like mad to fill it up again. For years this place was the command post of Staf, the co-founder of ACN, who helped to make it great and who dreamed of and built the warehouse. Here he hammered out new plans and dreamed up the most audacious arrangements during councils of war with his car and truck drivers: so as to make the miles shorter and the loading capacity of the trucks greater, to empty and to fill his warehouses, preferably at the same time, empty/full, empty/full, in an unceasing rhythm of zeal and love.

Cooking goes on in the kitchen the whole time, where first Rosa and Gusta and now Tamara, Simone, Joséke and Fineke rule the roost, providing the permanent staff and one group of volunteers after another with the meals that are essential when working at such a pace.

Day and night the ten- and twenty-tonners and the chapel-trucks drive in and out, the loading lift whizzes, the electric presses groan, the conveyor belt rattles—and, when not on duty, the weary volunteers snore.

Two thousand tons of gift parcels, rags, paper, shoes, bottles, motor tyres and other goods are each given their place in the depot: under the stilt-houses, on top of the office, next to the bedrooms, behind the kitchen, right up to the door of the room made of cardboard that serves me as my headquarters.

Here one can observe a swarm of young Mill Hill priests, Norbertines or red-capped White Fathers invade the halls to take a break from theology with some hard labour in the service of the Church in distress. Here, during the Hungarian crisis, the students of Louvain worked day and night in shifts of fifteen volunteers at a time. Here the girls of Flanders worked for months with painstaking care and cheerful hearts sorting medicines, sweets, food and clothing, packing them and sending them to the tortured East. Together with the girls who organised the lottery (Bingo, Lotto, etc.), the women who wrote the addresses in our file-card system and the permanent international staff of ACN secretaries, they lived in the "Magdeburg" hostel, a ramshackle dwelling rented in the village, which housed incredible numbers of female volunteers.

On the piles of parcels one can read addresses in all the languages of the East, tongue-twisting, unpronounceable

names of emigré pastors and persecuted priests behind
the Iron Curtain who are holding the fort in dangerous
outposts of the Kingdom of God and who are able to
reinforce their preaching of the Gospel with practical
relief—thanks to the generosity of our benefactors.

Here is the food department, with shelves groaning
under the weight of sardines, tinned milk, corned beef,
gingerbread and chocolate. In one corner looms a pale
pink mountain made up of boxes of Tirlemont lump-
sugar, monumental and everlasting, because the supply
is always greater than can be sent away. In the cooling
plant there are long rows of smoked sausages and succu-
lent hams, brought from East and West Flanders the day
before yesterday by the vans of mercy. A few steps
farther away one finds the sanctum of Pauline, where
she and her Italian compatriots of the *Focolarini* run the
parcel service. On an ancient sewing machine that was
given to us, they are busy stitching sixty sheets, urgently
needed by a seminary in the East. As in a draper's shop,
rolls and rolls of bright and dark materials are piled up
on the shelves, while shirts, trousers, stockings, shoes,
pullovers, blouses, skirts and aprons, all sorted according
to size, wait in apple-pie order until they are required.
The official notices and letters calling for help for the
most tragic cases are responded to by ACN with parcels
full of things that will astonish the poor.

Priests from the colleges of western Flanders come to
this warehouse every holiday with their pupils; each
week a new group competes with the others to break
the day-record of finished bales.

This is the kingdom of Staf and Fouche and Jan and
Miel, of Heinz and Stafke, Juul, Dietmar and Luigi, of

Franske and Franz, Sus and Sooi, Guy, George and Gust, Bill, Fené, Remi and Richard and all the sturdy fellows from East and West who have passed through these halls or have stayed here, and who would have neglected their health or their families if Father Kets, the manager, or I myself, had not sent them to bed on time, or shooed them off home.

In this warehouse live seminarians and students who are overworked or who need a change. Here one finds a meeting place with an ever-open door for oil-stained drivers, who step out of their trucks tired but happy, and are soon back on the road to Hungary, Berlin, Vienna or Flensburg, as if it were no more than a short Sunday afternoon trip. Here is the mailing department in the care of Frits, Ricardo, "Little Father" Van Haesenbroeck and Michael, which maintains the barrage of millions of copies of the "Mirror", with which Belgium, the Netherlands, Germany, Switzerland, Austria, France, Italy, England, Ireland and Australia are being continuously bombarded. Here is the card-index, with its hundreds of thousands of names and addresses that have to be checked, grouped and sorted. Here the generous responses of benefactors are carefully registered, letters of thanks dispatched, new begging letters composed and translated, telephone books copied, possible future benefactors traced and everything imaginable done to get prosperous Western Christianity to provide the funds indispensable for those who are entrusted to Aid to the Church in Need.

The mailing service, with its addressograph and the punching machines for making address plates, is also in the warehouse. Next, in the midst of calculating

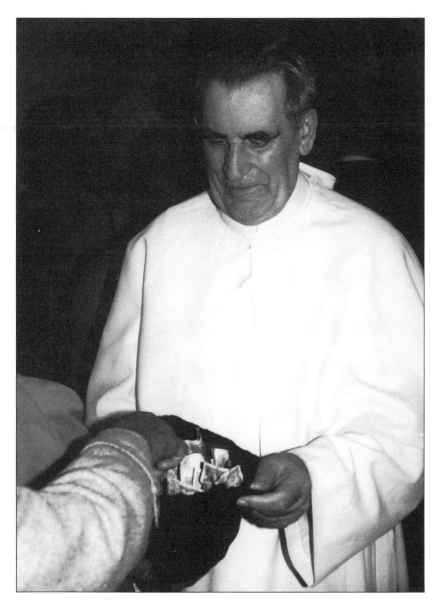

PLATE 32. Father Werenfried with his "hat of millions". In forty years he has collected and distributed an estimated two billion dollars.

machines and files, sits Mr. Lumens, the head of the bookkeeping department, as solid as if he were in a large chain-store business. Here are the budget department, with a dependable Hungarian as its chief; the jewellery service, where collected jewels are cleaned, repaired and sold; the exhibition hall, where one group of visitors after another is initiated with dash and imagination into the history, the purpose, the working methods and the necessity of Aid to the Church in Need, until they notice with dismay that their last dollar has gone on its way to the persecuted Church. Here is also my own office, with rattling typewriters, red-hot telephone lines, world atlases, dictaphones, piles of letters, folders, suitcases— and the remains of a hasty meal eaten just before leaving!

Nothing is unimportant here, nobody is superfluous: everyone can find a task in the service of this strange enterprise. Here Tuurke is sorting shoes, there Mr. Savate is checking the medicines. Here Miel keeps tabs on the number of bales in the warehouse and diners in the canteen. Over there Werner, the old submarine sailor, repaired amplifiers, film projectors and engines, until he disappeared just as mysteriously as he had come. Here Clément built stairs, dormitories and new offices with the same zeal he once put into building churches, houses and air-raid shelters. This was where Leo would restlessly hurry to and fro for his export licences, his work schedules, his transport service, always trying to stay on top of his temper—and his nerves. Here Mariette would fill in piles of forms for the collection service, for car insurance and for the cow run over by a chapel-truck. From this desk Germaine, small but intrepid, used to look after the office, the book-keeping and the preaching programme, arranging everything with clockwork precision and with all the willpower needed to keep this strange undertaking, and myself, in a minimum of order. She did it for years, mostly on her own.

Where are they now, those faithful souls who spent their best years here, the tough fellows fresh out of the Foreign Legion or prison, the idealists and the scatter-brained, the trouble-makers, embittered by sorrow and failure, the quarrellers and the drinkers, the talkers and the dreamers, the unselfish and the profiteers, the artists and the saints? These and many others helped, and some-times hindered us, to the best of their capacities, yet we could not have done without them, and we remain grate-ful for everything they did for love of the Church in need.

The warehouse calls up memories of the many helpers who came and went or who fell by the wayside, like good Father Vervinckt, the last of the Flemings, who with his joviality, his superiority at the billiard table, his common sense, his love of good meals, his weekly sermon and his unchallenged authority as an archer, suc-ceeded for years in keeping everything in its place and the many unstable assistants on an even keel.

ACN is not a normal business. It is a temporary cam-paign for, let us hope, a temporary emergency. No busi-ness enterprise could have been built up with such an exotic collection of male and female collaborators pour-ing into the warehouse from all parts of Flanders and of Europe. No firm would have survived with a staff like this. But with this band of poor sinners, among whom I gladly reckon myself, God was able to do an unbeliev-able amount of good and work miracles of love. To all of this, the warehouse bears witness!

That is why I am so fond of these wide halls, where the stones speak and the concrete is warm with love, where young people toil to make others happy, where joy is packed up in armfuls and carried off in triumph, where the sun is caught and loaded onto trucks to be taken into the darkness.

This is the warehouse of ACN in the shadow of the Abbey of Tongerlo, surrounded by a chaos of lorries and chapel-trucks coming and going, close by the white monks, the cows and pigs, in the middle of the quiet Flemish landscape. This is the beating heart of a young movement, the headquarters of love, genius and good will in the service of the Church in distress.

The bell chimes once more. The monks pass in white procession to the choir and a young priest, making the Sign of the Cross, sings with a clear voice *"Deus in adjutorium meum intende"*, the opening words of the solemn prayer sung seven times a day for the needs of the Universal Church.

A DEAD MAN LIVES ON

We had adorned the finest room of the Abbot's quarters with arum lilies and white carnations, and we had laid him out in state surrounded by flickering candle flames and praying monks from morning till night. Emilius Stalmans, Abbot of Tongerlo, had gone to his eternal rest. In his fifty-sixth year of life, the thirty-fifth of his monastic profession, the thirty-first of his priesthood and the sixteenth of his abbatial dignity, God took him from an abbey that was alive with prayer and buzzing with activity. He was taken away from the circle of his White sons, who had launched out from the altar of their profession into three continents, inspired by his enthusiasm, guided by his wisdom and borne up in his paternal heart.

He lay silent and tranquil, the expression of goodness unchanged upon his noble face. The hard cross lay between his folded hands and on his head a white, unadorned mitre. The crozier—the rod under which it was good to live—lay in his slightly bent arm. Above him the ancient cross with the glorious Christ, which had stood for centuries consolingly above dead prelates. At his feet the coat-of-arms with the good motto that he had never betrayed: *Multae misericordiae et verax*. Round about him were his fellow monks and the simple village people, his relatives and many friends, continually passing by to bless him and take their leave of him.

He was a great and noble man. Even as novice master he radiated an influence that had endured. He was the leader of Flemish youth in a wide radius around the grey walls of Tongerlo. With their banners emblazoned with the Flemish lion, with all their ideals they came to the old abbey to listen to him and to be understood by him. His spiritual lessons were like hammer-blows with which he forged his young monks—alas for only a few years—into the Paul of steel and the Norbert of granite so often on his lips.

Called to Rome, he became, in an international community, the warm heart and genius that bridged all contrasts, the kind father who became all things to all men. Since 1937 he had been our abbot, great, strong, understanding, broadminded, kind and good. He had an open mind for every new plan and for every daring enterprise. He trusted his monks. He forgot their faults and was proud of their achievements. He supported and blessed everything that was good, and did not fear to bear responsibility for what had been undertaken with his approval. Under his leadership there was a great increase of pioneers in our abbey, men who sought new ways and experimented, the young dare-devils of God's Kingdom. Never did he abandon one of them in the difficulties that all pioneer work inevitably entails.

Twice he went to Africa, to the missions, in order to understand the best of us in our superhuman apostolate. He prayed every day for new and holy monks so that he could fill up the depleted ranks of our missionaries. He was the moral support of our good Father van Clé in his restless apostolic zeal. He gave his blessing to the "Tower", the daring and honest magazine of the abbey

PLATE 33. Abbot Emilius Stalmans of Tongerlo.

which, in a time of cowardice and injustice, with *his* approval preached truth and love. He promoted the splendour of divine office, and blessed the liturgical apostolate that it gave rise to. He founded three monasteries and populated them with the best monks he could find. He was father abbot of two contemplative Norbertine convents which enjoyed his exceptional care.

It was he who charged me to put my life in the service of refugees and the persecuted. He was the wise chairman of Aid to the Church in Need, and he had the courage to open his eyes to reality. He shed tears in the bunker of Frankfurt, and knelt at my side before the Blessed Sacrament, in the wardrobe in an attic where a rucksack priest had his dwelling. He listened for hours to the tales of woe I had to tell and to the bold plans I laid before him for his approval. He threw all his moral authority into the balance to break the opposition to our work of charity. He loved, promoted, supported and defended Aid to the Church in Need right up to the last conversation I had with him two days before his unexpected death.

What a loss we have suffered! Dear Abbot Stalmans, how we burdened you with our cares! How we used up and wore out your great heart! What demands we made on your time, your love, your wisdom, your experience and your immense understanding—and not only we, but countless people outside the abbey. We knew quite well that your health was not good. But we needed you, and you kept yourself from no one. You never wanted to refuse a service. You would never let a poor wretch go uncomforted. You were all things to all men, until you had given yourself quite away. And then you were ripe for God.

You died on 13 April 1953, but your memory shall remain. Without you there would have been no Aid to the Church in Need. That is why your name must have its place on the first and last pages of this book. In the name of the refugees and the persecuted, I thank you that by the help of your paternal friendship we were permitted to begin this work. And we ask you to intercede with Almighty God so that we, in His strength and with His Blessing, may complete what was begun by you and by us.